Scott and Jim's Favorite Bike Rides

by
Scott Eltringham
and
Jim Wade

S&J Cycling

WARNING!!! Bicycling is an inherently dangerous activity. Use the information contained herein at your own risk. Many route descriptions may be vague and do not list all possible hazards. Also, all routes require on-street riding in traffic lanes, and some require riding sections of off-road terrain. You should be comfortable riding under all types of conditions before attempting any of these routes. Ride smart—wear a helmet at all times!

The cues, maps, or any other information contained herein (collectively, "the Rides") that S&J Cycling, Scott Eltringham, and/or James R. Wade (collectively "S&J Cycling") provide you are subject to the following Terms of Use.

S&J Cycling provides the Rides "As Is." S&J Cycling hereby disclaims all warranties and conditions with regard to the Rides, including all warranties and conditions of merchantability, whether express, implied or statutory, fitness for a particular purpose, title, and non-infringement. In no event shall S&J Cycling be liable for any injuries, death, damages, or property loss resulting directly or indirectly from using any information in the Rides. In no event shall S&J Cycling be liable for any special, indirect or consequential damages or any damages whatsoever, whether in an action of contract, negligence or other tortious action, arising out of or in connection with the use of the Rides, provision of or failure to provide services. S&J Cycling does not warrant that the Rides will be error-free or that defects will be corrected.

By purchasing, reading, or otherwise using the Rides, you indicate your complete and unconditional acceptance of these terms and conditions. If you do not agree to the terms and conditions of this agreement, do not make use of any of the information contained in the Rides. If any provision of this agreement is found to be unlawful or void then that provision shall be severed from this agreement and will not affect the validity of the remaining provisions.

The Rides are intended for the individual use of the purchaser. You may copy any map and cue sheet to carry with you on a ride. If riding with several people, you may make multiple printouts of that map and cue for use by your riding group. Except as provided above, you may not reproduce or redistribute the Rides (or copies) in any manner.

Cover photo: Rectortown Road just north of Rectortown, Virginia. Photo by Sally Wade.
Group photo on last page by Beth Cvrkel.

Second Edition, Second Printing
February 2007

Published by S&J Cycling
P.O. Box 41405
Arlington, VA 22204

ISBN 9-780977-071319

Ridden, Written, and Manufactured in the United States of America.

To our wives Sarah and Mary, for without them,
neither this book nor much of our riding would be possible,

To Michael Schlitzer, Marny Cvrkel, and Yolanda Chavis,
for their invaluable and unequalled support,

To Scott Coady and John Tegeris, for their inspirational fund-raising efforts,

And to our friends and teammates on Team Cholesterol.

Table of Contents

Foreword 7

Introduction 9
    Ride Summary Table 12
    Directions to Start Points 13

Multi-Use Trails 15
    1. Washington & Old Dominion 16
    2   Mount Vernon 18
    3   Capital Crescent 20
    4. Custis 22

Southern Maryland 23
    Description 25
    5. Indian Head 26

Frederick region 28
    Descriptions 29
    6. Some Flat from Frederick 32
    7. Catoctin Climber 34
    8. Around Antietam 36

Montgomery County region 39
    Descriptions 40
    10. Riley's Lock 48
    11. Riley's Lock #2 50
    12. MC Hammerfest 52
    13. Poolesville 54
    14. The Ferry Loop 56
    15. Backwards Poolesville 58
    16. Middletown Dreams 60
    17. Hill Climber's Delight 62

Nokesville region 65
    Descriptions 66
    20. Smutny's Delight 78
    21. West of Nokesville 80
    22. Nokesville #9 82
    23. Stafford Loop 84
    24. Rural Pleasures 86
    25. Some Hill in Nokesville 88
    26. Shooting the Breeze 90

31. Short Warrenton 92
32. East of Warrenton 94
33. Southern Views 96
34. Blue Ridge Views 98
35. King of Swain 100

The Plains region 103
Descriptions 104
40. Lovetts or Lees It 120
42. The Plains 122
43. Bulls on Parade 124
44. Spectacle Loop 126
45. Picnic from the Plains 128
46. Backwards Plains 130
47. Horse Hills 132
50. The Sammy Hagar Ride 134
51. No Plains, No Gains 136
52. The Gainesville 50 138
60. Tally Ho! 140
61. Bug, Sweat & Tears 142
62. The Marshall Plan 144
63. Stormin' the Gap 146
64. Piedmont Pig Ride 148
65. The Blue Ridger 150

About the Authors 152

Foreword

"During my racing career, I had the opportunity to train and race on many of the roads in the Northern Virginia and Central Maryland region. I remember well how beautiful and challenging the roads can be there—if you know where you're going. In this detailed and insightful guidebook, Scott Eltringham and Jim Wade have done the legwork for you, showcasing and categorizing a variety of great routes. Their passion for the sport is evident as they guide you towards many a scenic and challenging adventure.

"As many of you may know, off the bike, I have been on a challenging adventure of my own – battling Parkinson's disease. Subsequently, I've created the Davis Phinney Foundation in order to support curative research into Parkinson's Disease as well as promoting overall wellness and a positive outlook for people challenged by the disease. I am honored that Scott and Jim have pledged to donate the profits of this book to our foundation."

Davis Phinney, June 2005

Davis Phinney is credited as one of the winningest cyclists in U.S. history with over 300 victories, including two Tour de France stage wins and an Olympic bronze medal. Davis is married to Connie Carpenter (1984 Olympic Gold Medalist Road Race) and they have two children. They reside in Boulder, Colorado, and for over twenty years have run the renowned Carpenter/Phinney Bike Camps (bikecamp.com). For more information or donations call, write or visit them online:

Davis Phinney Foundation
P.O. Box 19264
Boulder, Colorado 80308
303-733-3340
www.davisphinneyfoundation.com

As of the date of the printing of this edition, we have raised over $6,000 for the Davis Phinney Foundation through sales of this book. We appreciate the contribution you made by purchasing this book. Thank you.

Introduction

You already know your answer to the question, "Why bike?" One answer is that bicycling lets you explore an area at a pace that is neither too fast nor too slow. Unlike traveling by car, you feel the sun on your face, smell the air, and taste the rain. But why drive to ride your bike? We have a number of answers to that, such as the desire for variety and a sense of exploration. But perhaps the best answer is that a healthy dose of rural calm at least once a month does a lot to soothe the urban frenzy of work, traffic and impatience. After riding in the countryside together for ten years, more weekends than not, we find the time invested in driving outside of the beltway to be one of the most worthwhile investments we have made.

For those occasions when we lack the time, a trail ride is a fair substitute. We have included information on four of the more significant bike trails in the area for just those times.

We organize most of the rides into four connected regions. The four trails and INDIAN HEAD (#5) are the only rides not included in this system. The two Maryland regions are divided generally on county lines, while the Virginia regions are split more on character: The Plains region is generally hillier and has a different "feel" to it than the Nokesville region. Within a region, we group the descriptions at the beginning, followed by the cues and maps. This system puts each cue sheet facing its map and makes for easier comparison of the profiles.

Since we live to the east of these regions, we start rides at the easternmost city and ride west. With one exception, all of our road rides are loops, which makes it very easy to start a ride from any city the ride passes through. The only ride that is not a loop is MIDDLETOWN DREAMS (#16), an out-and-back ride from Poolesville to Middletown in Maryland.

Mellow Rides

If you are new to bicycling or looking for a relatively mellow ride, we have several to suggest. The short version of RILEY'S LOCK is a great choice—25 miles long, and easy for most area cyclists to get to. All of the rides in the box at right feature light traffic for most of the ride and are not too hilly—all are in category I or II (see page 11 for an explanation of the categories).

Good "Starter" Rides	
10. Riley's Lock	25 mi
13. Poolesville	24 mi
21. Nokesville	30 mi
24. Rural Pleasures	30 mi
31. Short Warrenton	32 mi

Are You Tough Enough?

For those looking for something a little more difficult, we can offer several rides that will put your legs to the test. Of course, there's the classic Chuck & Gail ride THE BLUE RIDGER (#56), which has been a staple of cycling fanatics in this area for many, many years. Try that one or any of the other four in the box to the right. All of them are category V (our hardest), and AROUND ANTIETAM is almost *hors categorie*. We save these rides for the late summer or early fall when our fitness is at its peak. Even then, these rides hurt!

Five for the Fit	
7. Catoctin Climber	46 mi
8. Around Antietam	63 mi
34. Blue Ridge Views	60 mi
64. Piedmont Pig Ride	54 mi
65. The Blue Ridger	56 mi

Not Long Enough?

Although our maximum ride length is 64 miles, the picture below shows one set of connections between our northern-most and our southern-most routes. Three of our rides are good "bridges" between the regions: THE FERRY LOOP (#14) between The Plains and Montgomery County, MIDDLETOWN DREAMS (#16) connects Frederick and Montgomery County, and PICNIC FROM THE PLAINS (#45) bridges The Plains and Nokesville.

Route Variations

When a route has variations, the "main" route is the first one listed on the cue. On the map, it is the solid line. Alternate routes are shown by dashed lines on the map when using different roads. On the cue, a left-pointing finger on the main ride notes the point where the alternate route departs from the main route. A right-pointing finger notes the point where the alternate route rejoins the main route (if it does). The first variation has one asterisk. If the ride has two variations, the second one has two asterisks.

Legend	
7.	Catoctin Climber
8.	Around Antietam
16.	Middletown Dreams
14.	The Ferry Loop
40.	Lovetts or Lees It
47.	Horse Hills
42.	The Plains
45.	Picnic from the Plains
24.	Rural Pleasures
23.	Stafford Loop

Numbering System

We numbered the rides as we did for two reasons: to keep rides in the same region together and to leave room for expansion. When we began this project several years ago, we numbered each new ride consecutively. Over time, this led to one Gainesville ride being numbered in the 30's and another in the 40's. Renumbering them once was enough, we decided, and left room to keep growing.

Suggested Use

We prefer the single-page cue and single-page map format for ease of reading. If you print both the cue and the map at 50% scale, trim the white space, put them back-to-back and laminate them, you have a handy cue card that is protected from rain and sweat. At that size, it fits nicely into a jersey pocket or a clip taped to your stem.

How We Started

A major source of inspiration for this book was Chuck and Gail Helfer's book, *Chuck & Gail's Favorite Bicycle Rides* (1992). Scott bought one of the last copies that his local bike store had in 1996. The rides in that book showed him just how beautiful this area is and we have spent hundreds of hours experiencing those rides. Chuck and Gail allowed us to "steal" their format and to use several of their rides in this book. We changed the names of many of their rides in accord with our sense of humor, but we rarely needed or wanted to change the routes. It is a testament to their planning that many of their rides are still wonderful rides fifteen years after the date of their last publication.

Route Ratings

I	Basically flat and not too long
II	A few small hills, but nothing major
III	Generally rolling terrain with a few decent climbs
IV	Rolling throughout – expect very little flat and generally challenging terrain
V	Rolling throughout plus either a major climb or a longer distance

Cue Abbreviations

L	Left Turn
R	Right Turn
BL	Bear to the Left
BR	Bear to the Right
SS	Stop sign
SL	Stop light
X	Cross intersection
S	Continue Straight. Usually used at an intersection often with a road name change
TRO	To Remain On. The route makes a turn but the road name or number stays the same
B/c	Becomes. Notes a change in the road name or number but no turn necessary
☹	Use Caution: relatively bad traffic

Map Symbols

▬▬▬	Main route	▢	Relatively major road
▬ ▬ ■	Route variation	◯	Relatively minor road
———	Paved road (when last we checked)	★	City or town (sometimes very small)
- - - -	Unpaved road (when last we checked)		

Table 1. Ride Summary

#	Start	Name	Distance	Category
1	--	W&OD Trail	45	--
2	--	Mount Vernon Trail	18	--
3	--	Capital Crescent Trail	11	--
4	--	Custis Trail	4	--
5	Indian Head	Indian Head	23, 37 or 41	II
6	Frederick	Some Flat from Frederick	45	II
7	Frederick	Catoctin Climber	46 or 47	V
8	Frederick	Around Antietam	63	V
10	Riley's Lock	Riley's Lock	25 or 38	II
11	Riley's Lock	Riley's Lock #2	43	III
12	Riley's Lock	MC Hammerfest	47 or 51	III
13	Poolesville	Poolesville	24, 35 or 42	II/III
14	Poolesville	The Ferry Loop	44	III
15	Poolesville	Backwards Poolesville	51	III
16	Poolesville	Middletown Dreams	57 or 61	IV
17	Point of Rocks	Hill Climber's Delight	30 or 40	IV/V
20	Nokesville	Smutny's Delight	31 or 39	I
21	Nokesville	(West of) Nokesville	30 or 43	I
22	Nokesville	Nokesville #9	43	I
23	Nokesville	Stafford Loop	46 or 52	II
24	Calverton	Rural Pleasures	30 or 48	I
25	Nokesville	Some Hill in Nokesville	64	II
26	Calverton	Shooting the Breeze	39	III
31	Warrenton	Short Warrenton	32	II
32	Warrenton	East of Warrenton	43, 52 or 58	II
33	Warrenton	Southern Views	54	IV
34	Warrenton	Blue Ridge Views	60	V
35	Warrenton	King of Swain	41	IV
40	Leesburg	Lovetts or Lees It	43	III
42	The Plains	The Plains	34 or 39	III
43	The Plains	Bulls on Parade	35 or 38	IV
44	The Plains	Spectacle Loop	44	IV
45	The Plains/Gainesville	Picnic from the Plains	44 or 54	III
46	The Plains	Backwards Plains	51 or 60	III
47	Middleburg/The Plains	Horse Hills	43 or 59	IV
50	Gainesville	The Sammy Hagar Ride	39	III
51	Gainesville	No Plains, No Gains	42	IV
52	Gainesville	The Gainesville 50	50	IV
60	Marshall/The Plains	Tally Ho!	38 or 50	IV
61	Marshall	Bug, Sweat & Tears	43 or 55	IV
62	Marshall	The Marshall Plan	39	III
63	Marshall	Stormin' the Gap	47 or 55	IV
64	Marshall	Piedmont Pig Ride	54	V
65	Marshall	The Blue Ridger	51 or 56	V

Directions to Start Points

H.M. Pearson ElemeAntary School in **Calverton**: Take I-66 west to exit 44, route 234 S. Go 5.3 miles and take exit for route 28 S. Go 11.75 miles and turn right on route 603. Go 0.9 mile and turn right into the school.

Waverly Elementary School in **Frederick**: Take I-270 north to Frederick. After about 30 miles, continue on US-40. After just over a mile, take exit 13B US-40/SR-144/W. Patrick St. Go 1.3 miles and turn right on Waverly Drive. In 0.6 mile, turn left into the school.

Municipal parking lot in **Frederick**: Take I-270 north to Frederick. After about 30 miles, continue on US-40. After just over a mile, take exit 13B US-40/SR-144/W. Patrick St. Go through the "golden mile." At the junction which has route 40 to the right and I-70 to the left, stay right on route 40W (towards Gambrill State Park). Go up the hill. The lot is just east of the Dan-Dee Motel, near where you see Gambrill Park Rd on the right.

Tyler Elementary School in **Gainesville**: Take I-66 west to exit 43A, route 29 south in Gainesville. Turn right at the first stop light, route 55 (John Marshall Highway). Go about 1 mile and turn right into the school.

Smallwood State Park (**Indian Head**): Take I-95 to route 210 south, Indian Head Highway. Go 14.0 miles and turn left on route 227 at the light. In 1.4 miles go straight onto route 224. At the T, turn left on routes 225/224, and then turn right in 0.4 mile to stay on route 224. Go 4 miles and turn right on Sweden Point Road into the state park. In 0.3 mile turn right at the bottom of the hill toward the boat ramp. Turn right into the first lot by the ranger station. At times, the Park charges a use fee. See http://www.dnr.state.md.us/publiclands/southern/smallwood.html for more information.

Loudoun County High School, 415 Dry Mill Rd., SW, in **Leesburg**: Take I-66 west to exit 67, the Dulles Toll Road, VA-267. Go 28 miles. Take the US-15 S/VA-7 W exit (number 1A) on the left towards Leesburg/Warrenton. Go 0.8 mile and take the first exit, US-15 Bus. Turn right at the end of the exit. Go 0.4 mile and turn left on Catoctin Circle Drive (the second light). Go 0.6 mile to the intersection with Dry Mill Rd. The school is on the left.

Community Center in **Marshall**: Take I-66 west to exit 28 (Marshall). At the end of the exit, turn right (north). Go about half a mile to the stoplight in Marshall. Go straight at the stoplight. The community center is on the right just past the intersection.

Middleburg Elementary School in Middleburg: Take I-66 west to exit 31 (The Plains). At the end of the exit, turn right (north) to the stop sign in The Plains, about a mile. Turn right at the stop sign. Take the next left on route 626, just after the gas station. Go 8 miles to Middleburg. Turn right on route 50 at the T and then left onto route 626, Madison St, at the stoplight. Go 0.1 mile and turn right into the school.

Nokesville Community Park in Nokesville: Take I-66 west to exit 44, route 234 S. Go 5.3 miles and take exit for route 28 S. Go 4.75 miles and turn left on 652 at the light. Go 1 mile (through Nokesville) and turn right on Aden Rd at the T. Go 0.75 mile and turn right into the park (the entrance is just past the first small hill on Aden Rd). The Park may be closed from October 31 through March 30.

The Plains: Take I-66 west to exit 31 (The Plains). At the end of the exit, turn right (north) to the stop sign in The Plains, about a mile. Turn right at the stop sign. Take the next left on route 626, just after the gas station. Again, take the next left, just before the railroad tracks, and park.

Point of Rocks Train Station in Point of Rocks, Md: Take I-270 north to exit 6B, route 28 west. Go 27.8 miles on route 28 to Point of Rocks. The railroad station is on your left as you enter the town.

Poolesville High School in Poolesville: Take I-495 to the River Road exit, route 190 west. This exit is the second one after crossing into Maryland from Virginia. Go 11 miles to the T. Turn left to remain on River Rd. Go 1.4 miles and turn right on Partnership Rd. In 3.8 miles, turn left on 107, Whites Ferry Rd. Go 2.5 mile and turn left on West Willard Rd at the stop sign. Go 0.25 mile and turn left into the first parking lot.

Riley's Lock (on the C&O Canal in Seneca, Md.): Take I-495 to the River Road exit, route 190 West. This exit is the second one after crossing into Maryland from Virginia. Go 11 miles to the T. Turn left to remain on River Rd. Go 0.5 mile and turn left on Riley's Lock Rd. Go about 0.5 mile and turn left into the first parking lot, across from the second boat launch ramp.

Municipal parking lot in **Warrenton**: Take I-66 west to exit 43A, route 29 South in Gainesville. Go 11.5 miles and take the exit for Business 29/15 Warrenton/Luray—it's a big sweeping exit to the right. Go 0.8 mile and turn left at the first stoplight (Blackwell Rd). Go 1 mile to the T and turn right on Main St. Make an immediate left on Ashby. Go straight for a block and straight into the parking lot.

Multi-Use Trails

The greater D.C. area is blessed with several excellent trails. Although we generally prefer the open roads outside the Beltway, the trails provide good options to get some miles in without the need to drive too far to the start point. Better yet, for many people, one of these trails will be close enough to their homes to dispense with the need for a car altogether!

A word of warning: Riding on trails has its own unique dangers. Wear a helmet and stop at all street crossings! Visibility is often less open than when on a road, particularly to the sides. Watch for dogs on leashes, dogs not on leashes and people suddenly stepping onto the trail from the bushes, to name just a few of the hazards commonly encountered on these trails.

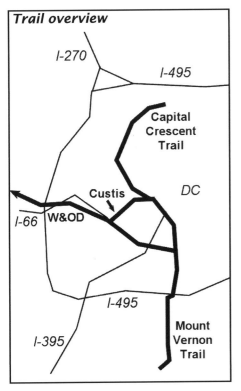

Trail overview

The overview map at left shows four of the major trails of the area. We showcase these four in the following pages:

- Washington & Old Dominion
- Mount Vernon
- Capital Crescent
- Custis

Washington & Old Dominion (W&OD) Trail. The W&OD is a 45-mile multi-use rail-to-trail built on the former Washington & Old Dominion Railroad. It runs through the urban heartland and countryside of Northern Virginia, from Shirlington near I-395 to Purcellville in Loudoun County.

Mount Vernon Trail. Built by the National Park Service back in 1973, the 18-mile Mount Vernon Trail parallels the Potomac River and the George Washington Parkway between Roosevelt Island and Mount Vernon. It also connects to the Custis and W&OD trails on the east.

Capital Crescent Trail. Another rails-to-trails project, it runs through Northwest D.C. to Silver Spring, Maryland. The southern 7 miles (Georgetown to Bethesda) have a wide asphalt surface and are in excellent condition. The northern Georgetown Branch extension has a crushed gravel surface for the final 4 miles between Bethesda and Silver Spring.

Custis Trail. The Custis Trail runs along I-66 in Arlington County and is protected by noise walls. Extending from Roosevelt Island to mile 4 of the W&OD it provides good access to D.C.

Maps on the Web

Northern Virginia trails www.fhiplan.com/novabike/

Arlington www.bikearlington.com/bikemaps.cfm

Alexandria www.alexride.org/images/bikemap.pdf

D.C. www.ddot.dc.gov/ddot/cwp/view,a,1245,q,629849,ddotNav,|32399|.asp

Fairfax www.co.fairfax.va.us/nmtc/maps.html

MC gis.montgomerycountymd.gov/ims/bikeways/viewer.htm

1. Washington & Old Dominion Trail

The longest paved trail in the area and our personal favorite is the W&OD. Beginning in Shirlington, stretching all the way to Purcellville, and paved the entire way, the trail is a great way to get in a quick bit of saddle time when your day is full and you want to minimize travel time to the start. The sections close to the major suburbs get crowded on nice days, but generally return to a less congested state within a mile or so outside of each town. End-to-end distance is just over 45 miles, or 90 miles if you do the whole trail at once.

The eastern ten miles of the trail can be a little annoying due to the large number of street crossings. It is not until about mile 10 that the trail has good stretches of unbroken pavement. The two-mile stretches on both sides of Vienna are a nice taste of the open trail to the west. Just past Herndon at mile 20, the street crossings pick up again, but only briefly.

A giant quarry is just to the south of the trail at mile 30. At mile 33, the trail cuts underneath the Route 15 Leesburg Bypass. This underpass has several sharp turns with limited sight distance. Be careful please. The last 15 miles of the trail (towards Purcellville) are particularly beautiful and include sections where the trees provide a natural canopy of shade—a welcome feature on hot, sticky D.C. summer days!

Length	45.0 miles, all paved.
Water	2.5, 3.3, 4.0, 11.6, 16.6, 20.0, 22.5 & 34.0 mi
Ends	*East*: Just west of I-395 at the intersection of Glebe Road and Four Mile Run by the Village at Shirlington Shopping Center.
	West: Purcellville, Virginia on 21st St N one block north of route 7.
Metro	*East Falls Church*: Next to trail at mile 5.0.
	Dunn Loring: The station is 0.75 miles south of trail at mile 9.5 via Gallows Road.
	Vienna: The station is 1.5 miles south of trail at mile 10.5 via Route 123.
	Bikes are allowed on all Metrorail cars on weekends and during non-rush hour weekday periods, except during special events.
Links	*Mount Vernon Trail*: To continue east to the Potomac and the Mount Vernon trail, use the pedestrian overpass located about 2 blocks south of the trail head at 28th St. S. and S. Quincy Street. Once across, turn left (north) on Martha Custis Drive. Bear left when it merges with Valley Drive. At the stoplight at West Glebe Road go left. The Four Mile Run trail begins to your right at the next stoplight at S. Glebe Road. It joins the Mount Vernon Trail just south of National Airport.
	Custis Trail: At mile 4.0, the W&OD intersects with the western end of Custis Trail. A covered bench and a drinking fountain mark that intersection.

On the Web

General
www.wodfriends.org
bikewashington.org/trails/
 wad/wad.htm

Parking
www.wodfriends.org/parking.html

Maps
www.wodfriends.org/map1.html

1. W&OD Trail

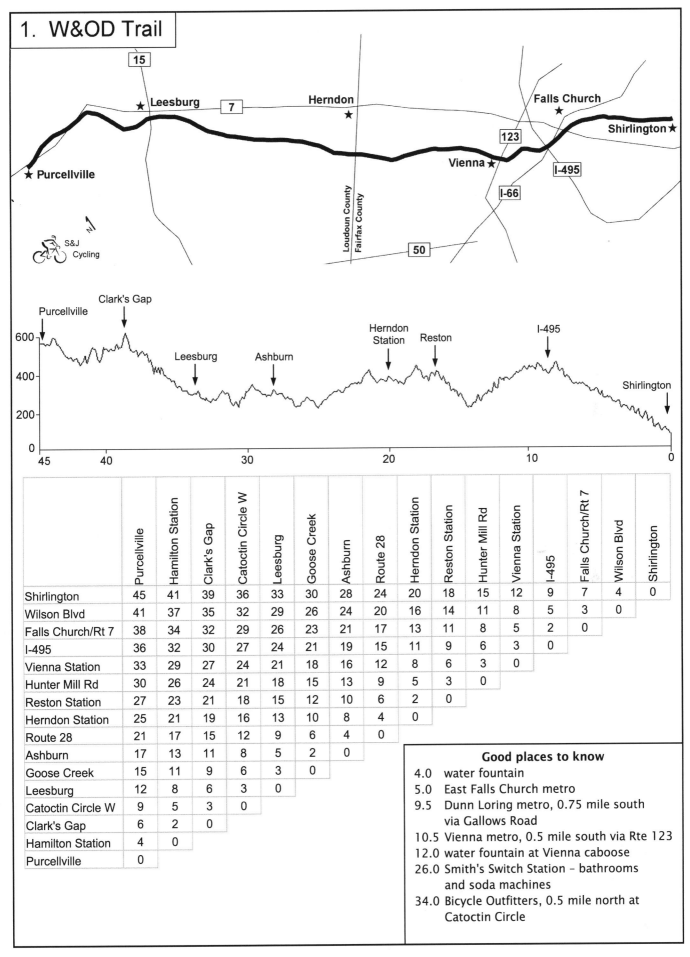

	Purcellville	Hamilton Station	Clark's Gap	Catoctin Circle W	Leesburg	Goose Creek	Ashburn	Route 28	Herndon Station	Reston Station	Hunter Mill Rd	Vienna Station	I-495	Falls Church/Rt 7	Wilson Blvd	Shirlington
Shirlington	45	41	39	36	33	30	28	24	20	18	15	12	9	7	4	0
Wilson Blvd	41	37	35	32	29	26	24	20	16	14	11	8	5	3	0	
Falls Church/Rt 7	38	34	32	29	26	23	21	17	13	11	8	5	2	0		
I-495	36	32	30	27	24	21	19	15	11	9	6	3	0			
Vienna Station	33	29	27	24	21	18	16	12	8	6	3	0				
Hunter Mill Rd	30	26	24	21	18	15	13	9	5	3	0					
Reston Station	27	23	21	18	15	12	10	6	2	0						
Herndon Station	25	21	19	16	13	10	8	4	0							
Route 28	21	17	15	12	9	6	4	0								
Ashburn	17	13	11	8	5	2	0									
Goose Creek	15	11	9	6	3	0										
Leesburg	12	8	6	3	0											
Catoctin Circle W	9	5	3	0												
Clark's Gap	6	2	0													
Hamilton Station	4	0														
Purcellville	0															

Good places to know

4.0 water fountain
5.0 East Falls Church metro
9.5 Dunn Loring metro, 0.75 mile south
    via Gallows Road
10.5 Vienna metro, 0.5 mile south via Rte 123
12.0 water fountain at Vienna caboose
26.0 Smith's Switch Station – bathrooms
    and soda machines
34.0 Bicycle Outfitters, 0.5 mile north at
    Catoctin Circle

2. Mount Vernon Trail

The Mount Vernon Trail is a great multi-use recreation trail on the Virginia side of the Potomac River. Stretching for nearly 18 miles, the trail runs from Theodore Roosevelt Island to Mount Vernon, the site of George Washington's estate. It connects to the Custis trail at its northern end and to the Four Mile Run trail at the southern end of National Airport. The trail is well loved by area cyclists. On nice weekends, expect a high traffic volume of cyclists, runners, and walkers of all types. The trail offers wonderful views of the Potomac. Sights to see along the way include George Washington's home at Mount Vernon, Old Town Alexandria, and Gravelly Point, at the north end of National Airport's main runway.

This trail is one of the oldest trails in the area and the surface, while paved, may leave a little to be desired. The better pavement is generally found in the northern half; as you head south the trail takes more frequent twists and turns and increases in bumpiness. A number of recent projects have improved the trail substantially, such as the installation of two new overpasses. Some of the bridge crossings are very narrow, so consider dismounting your bike.

The trail has two route choices through Alexandria, both on the street. The older route follows Pitt Street through town. The newer "river route" is the better choice (please see detail map on facing page). This route follows Union Street, which provides easy access to the waterfront. Overall, you probably don't want the Mt. Vernon trail if you're looking for some speed work, but it is fine for a more leisurely ride where you can actually enjoy the sites and sounds of the city.

Length	18 miles. Paved wih sections of boardwalk in swamp areas. Narrow in areas.
Water	Multiple, see map.
Ends	*North:* Theodore Roosevelt Island on the Potomac River near Rosslyn, Va. By car, Roosevelt Island is accessible only by traveling northbound on the George Washington Memorial Parkway.
	South: Mount Vernon Estate in Virginia, home of George Washington.
Metro	*Rosslyn:* Exit the station and go one block east. Turn left on North Lynn Street. Turn right onto bike trail immediately after highway exit ramp. Cross over the George Washington Memorial Parkway on a bicycle bridge to the Roosevelt Island parking lot.
	National Airport, Arlington Cemetery, King Street and *Braddock Road* stops are all near or on the trail.
Links	*Custis Trail:* Continue north from Roosevelt Island. Follow the footbridge over the GW Parkway. Just ahead is the intersection of Lee Highway and Lynn Street in Rosslyn. The Custis trail begins here.
	Rock Creek Trail: Cross Memorial Bridge on the north side. Go left at the first street crossing.

On the Web

General
bikewashington.org/trails/vernon/vernon.htm

Maps
www.nps.gov/gwmp/mvtmap.html

Mount Vernon Estate
www.mountvernon.org

---

2. Mount Vernon Trail

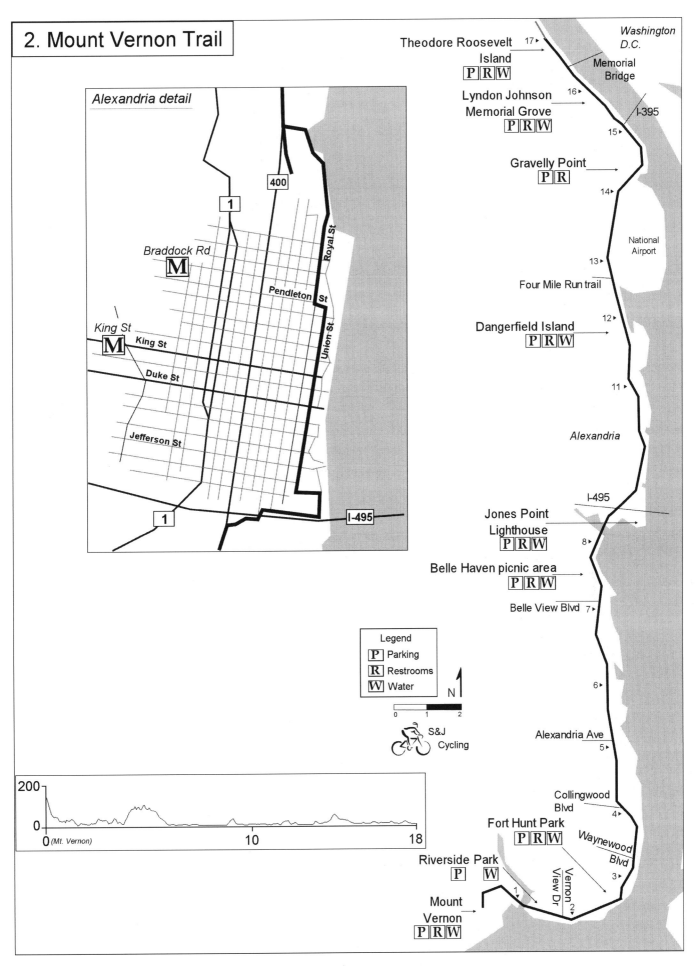

Alexandria detail

Braddock Rd **M**

King St **M** King St

Duke St

Jefferson St

1

1

400

Royal St

Pendleton St

Union St

I-495

Theodore Roosevelt
Island
P **R** **W**

Washington
D.C.

Memorial
Bridge

17►

Lyndon Johnson
Memorial Grove
P **R** **W**

16►

I-395

15►

Gravelly Point
P **R**

14►

National
Airport

13►

Four Mile Run trail

Dangerfield Island
P **R** **W**

12►

11►

Alexandria

I-495

Jones Point
Lighthouse
P **R** **W**

8►

Belle Haven picnic area
P **R** **W**

Belle View Blvd 7►

6►

Alexandria Ave

5►

Collingwood
Blvd

4►

Fort Hunt Park
P **R** **W**

Waynewood
Blvd

3►

Riverside Park
P **W**

Vernon
View Dr

Mount
Vernon
P **R** **W**

1►

2►

Legend

P Parking
R Restrooms
W Water

N

0   1   2

S&J
Cycling

200

0

0 (Mt. Vernon)   10   18

3. Capital Crescent Trail

Built on the corridor of the old Georgetown Branch railroad, the Capital Crescent Trail (CCT) is a recent addition to the region's collection of trails. Extending from Georgetown to Silver Spring, the southern seven miles are paved and the final four miles between Bethesda and Silver Spring have a crushed gravel surface. The paved portion of the Capital Crescent Trail is heavily traveled by cyclists and other recreational users—please be careful.

From Georgetown, the first three miles follow the Potomac River and the C & O Canal. The CCT then crosses Canal Road and heads north, moving away from the Potomac. Many of the busier street crossings now have overpasses. The paved section ends at Bethesda Ave., two blocks west of Wisconsin Ave. As the elevation profile shows, this section has a gradual uphill climb.

From Bethesda, the CCT passes through the Wisconsin Avenue Tunnel and changes to a crushed gravel surface. This section, called the Georgetown Branch extension, is best ridden on a mountain or hybrid bike.

Length	11 miles, northern 4 miles not paved.
Water	miles 3.5 (rest stop), 6.5 (rest stop) and 11.0 (past Jack's boathouse).
Restroom	mile 8.0 (Fletcher's Boathouse).
Ends	*Georgetown:* Western end of K Street NW (under Whitehurst Freeway and Key Bridge).
	Bethesda: Bethesda Avenue near Woodmont Ave., by Ourisman Honda.
	Silver Spring: Stewart Avenue, a half block south of Brookville Road.
Metro	*Silver Spring:* Directly across Colesville Road from the station exit.
	Bethesda: Exit the station at the rear and go south (left) on Woodmont Ave. The CCT is four blocks south on Woodmont, at Bethesda Avenue.
	Rosslyn: Take Lynn Street north from the station to Key Bridge. Use the bike path on the east side of the bridge, then turn right at the Maryland end of the bridge and follow the path down to the C&O Canal towpath and then down the staircase to Water Street. The CCT begins at the west end of Water Street.
Links	*Rock Creek Trail:* From the southern end of the CCT, go 0.9 miles east on K St.
	Mount Vernon and *Custis Trails:* Go 0.5 miles south over Key Bridge to Rosslyn Circle.

On the Web

General
www.cctrail.org
bikewashington.org/trails/
  cct/cct.htm

Parking
www.cctrail.org/CCT_Directions
  .htm#parking

Maps
www.cctrail.org/CCT_Maps.htm

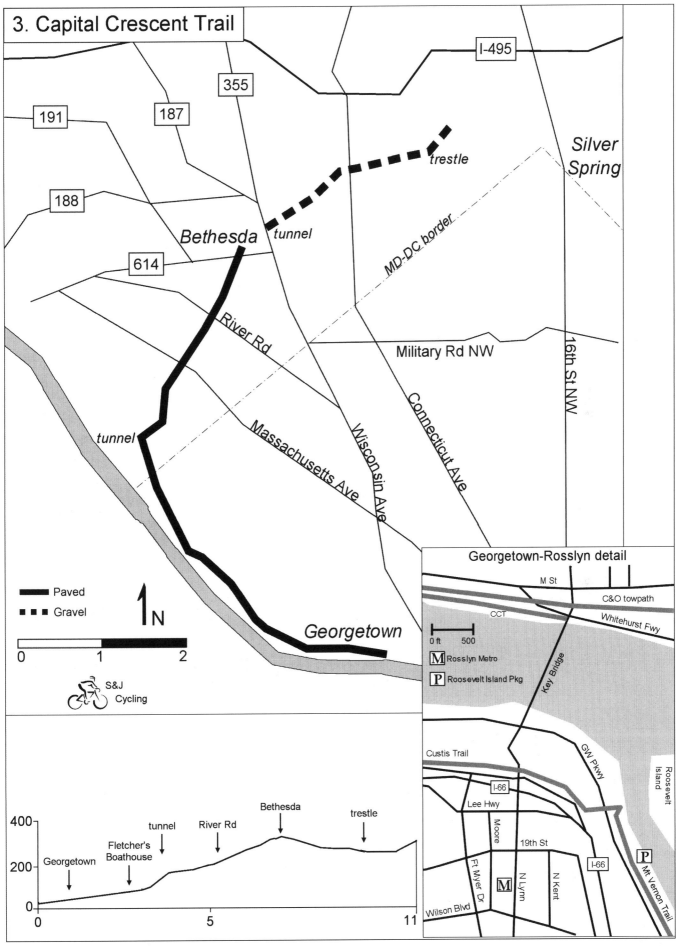

3. Capital Crescent Trail

I-495

355

191

187

188

614

Bethesda

tunnel

trestle

MD-DC border

Silver Spring

River Rd

Military Rd NW

Connecticut Ave

Wisconsin Ave

16th St NW

tunnel

Massachusetts Ave

Paved
Gravel

N

0   1   2

S&J Cycling

Georgetown

Georgetown-Rosslyn detail

M St

C&O towpath

CCT

Whitehurst Fwy

0 ft   500

M Rosslyn Metro
P Roosevelt Island Pkg

Key Bridge

GW Pkwy

Roosevelt Island

Custis Trail

I-66

Lee Hwy

Moore

19th St

I-66

P

Mt Vernon Trail

Ft Myer Dr

M

N Lynn

N Kent

Wilson Blvd

400

200

0

Georgetown

Fletcher's Boathouse

tunnel

River Rd

Bethesda

trestle

0   5   11

4. Custis Trail

The Custis Trail runs for four miles from Rosslyn to Falls Church. The Custis is not a rail-to-trail like the Washington & Old Dominion, but rather the result of good planning when I-66 was constructed. On the positive side, this means the trail has many fewer road crossings—only three in near the eastern end—but it also means that he trail is a little hillier and windier in some places.

The eastern end of the Custis Trail begins in Rosslyn as a wide sidewalk along the north side of Lee Highway. After passing the Key Bridge Marriott (be careful of crossing traffic here), the surface changes to asphalt. At the top of the following small climb, cross over I-66, and then go right to remain on the trail and following the interstate. Almost at the western end of the trail is a turn. When eastbound, almost immediately after turning onto the trail, you will come to a three-way path intersection. Go left to pass under I-66. The trail continues along the north side of the interstate. When westbound, go right at the stop sign when the trail passes under I-66.

Length	4 miles, all paved.
Water	Mile 4.0 at junction with W&OD Trail.
Ends	*West:* At mile 4.0 of the W&OD. A covered bench and a drinking fountain are at this intersection.

On the Web

General
bikewashington.org/trails/wad/custis.htm

Mileage chart
www.rundc.com/Trails/VA/Custis.htm

East: The intersection of Lee Highway and Lynn Street in Rosslyn, Virginia.

Metro — *Rosslyn:* Take Lynn Street north from the station to Lee Highway, about 1.5 blocks.

Links — *W&OD:* At the western end of the Custis Trail.

Mount Vernon Trail: From the eastern end, follow the path down the hill and across the footbridge over the George Washington Memorial Parkway to the parking lot for Roosevelt Island. The Mount Vernon Trail continues at the south end of the parking lot.

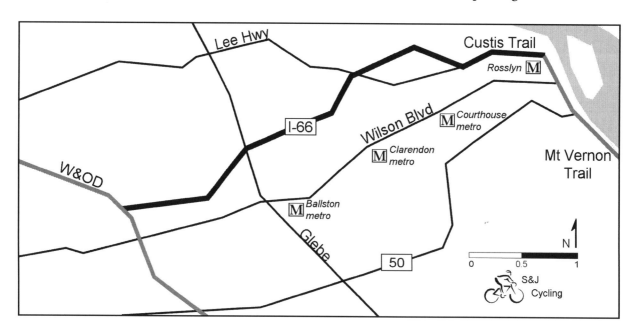

Southern Maryland

Calling this area a "region" would be a stretch, given that we only have one ride there, although with three distance options. We both enjoy the area, but if you live in the deep suburbs of Northern Virginia, this start point is probably the farthest away. The area is quite beautiful and generally flat, with most roads featuring light traffic and good pavement.

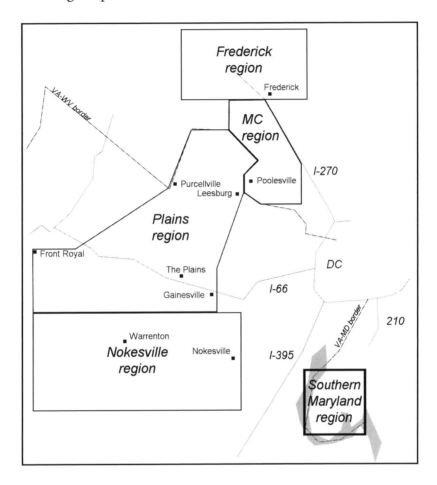

5. Indian Head

Distance *mi*	23.0	37.1	40.7
Category	II	II	II
Climbing *ft*	1353	1975	2200
Rel. climb *ft/mi*	58.8	53.2	54.1

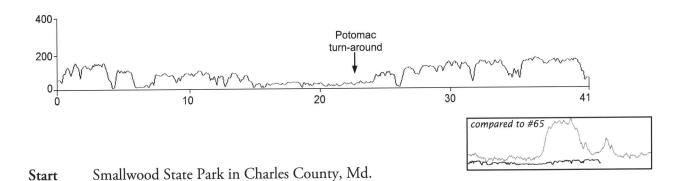

Start   Smallwood State Park in Charles County, Md.

Route   This ride—our only one in southern Maryland—rewards the effort spent driving to the start point with different scenery and long stretches of great pavement with few cars. The opening ten miles feature rolling hills, but the ride flattens out in the middle stretch. The Potomac turn-around makes an excellent place for a stretch break, offering a great view of the river.

Notes   While the distance to the ride start from Northern Virginia deters us from doing this ride very often, it has become a traditional "New Year's" ride for us on that one weekend in January where the temperatures become unseasonable mild. That's not a guarantee each year in the D.C. area, but watch the forecasts and be ready to get in some easy miles to start off your new year if the opportunity presents itself!

This area used to feature an abundance of dogs (seven different dogs chased our friend Dave on one memorable ride several years ago). Sadly, in recent times, even the sound of a distant dog barking has been all too scarce.

A Chuck & Gail ride.

5. Indian Head

Distance:	23, 37 or **41** miles
Rating:	II
Start:	Smallwood State Park in Charles County, Md.

41 Mile Ride

0.0	L	from parking toward park entrance		30.2	S	Durham Church Rd (bad curve in 1 mile!)
0.3	L	Sweden Point Rd at T		31.7	R	6 at T
0.6	R	224 at SS		32.6	L	Annapolis Woods Rd
5.5 ☞*	R	224 at 344		35.5	L	Poorhouse Rd
20.4	R	6 at T		37.6	S	484, Bicknell Rd
21.1		arrive at Potomac; turn around		39.2	L	Sweetman Rd
21.8	S	6 at 224		40.1	S	Sweden Point Rd into park
26.8 ☞**	R	425		40.4	R	toward boat ramp at bottom of hill
				40.7	R	to parking

*23 Mile Ride

10.2	L	Liverpool Point Rd; b/c Baptist Church Rd		14.5	L	425 at T. Join 37-mile ride in 1.6 miles at 30.2 turn

**37 Mile Ride

30.2	L	425 at Durham Church Rd		36.5	L	Sweden Point Rd into park
31.6	S	425 at 6		36.8	R	toward boat ramp at bottom of hill
31.7	L	Smallwood Church Rd		37.1	R	to parking
35.9	R	224 at T				

5. Indian Head

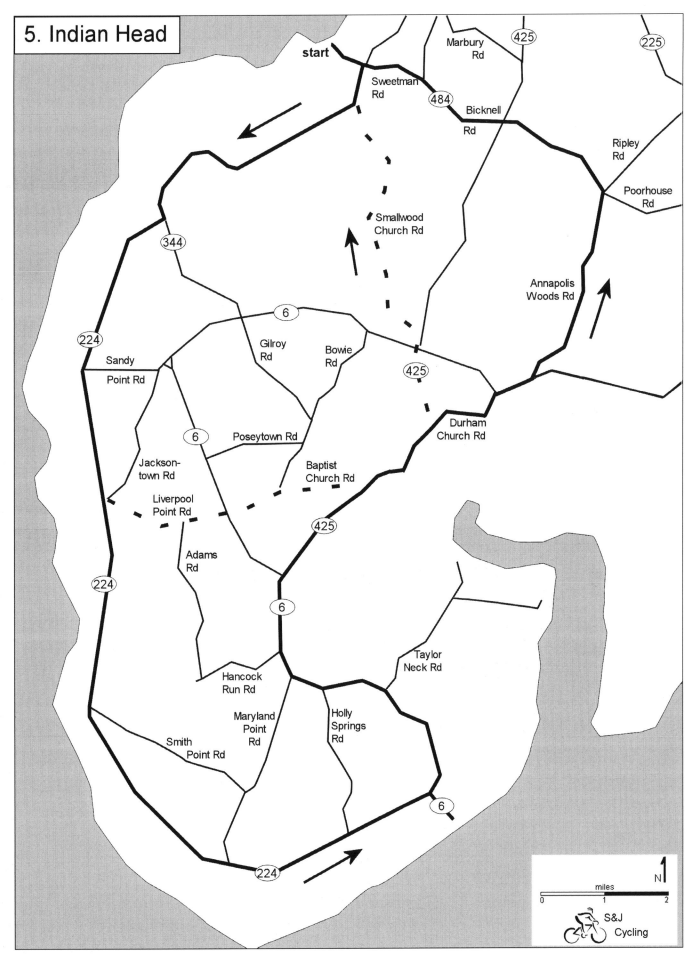

start

Marbury Rd

425

225

Sweetman Rd

484

Bicknell Rd

Ripley Rd

Poorhouse Rd

Smallwood Church Rd

344

Annapolis Woods Rd

6

224

Gilroy Rd

Bowie Rd

425

Sandy Point Rd

Durham Church Rd

6

Poseytown Rd

Jackson-town Rd

Baptist Church Rd

Liverpool Point Rd

425

224

Adams Rd

6

Taylor Neck Rd

Hancock Run Rd

Maryland Point Rd

Holly Springs Rd

Smith Point Rd

6

224

N

miles
0   1   2

S&J Cycling

Frederick region

"Frederick … Catoctin Mountain … Harp Hill … pain," went our thinking in the early days. The short version of CATOCTIN CLIMBER was the first ride we ever did from Frederick. If the area weren't so beautiful, it might have been our last. In climbing feet per mile, the 46-mile version of CATOCTIN CLIMBER is our hardest by a significant margin and the only one in triple digits.

We later added AROUND ANTIETAM and could then debate which of the two rides was harder. Move east of 15, however, and you are in a totally different world of gentle hills and sunshine. Our three main rides there are enough to keep us satisfied with variety and humble.

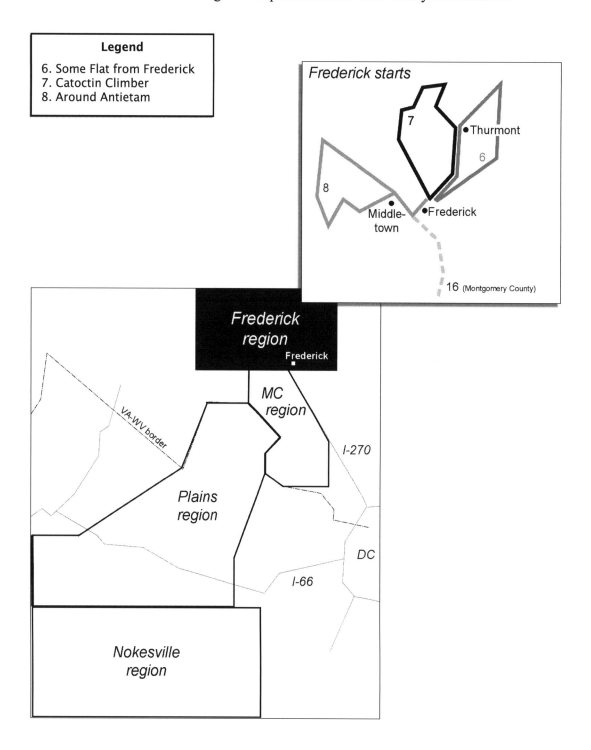

Legend

6. Some Flat from Frederick
7. Catoctin Climber
8. Around Antietam

Frederick starts

7

•Thurmont

6

8

Middle-town

•Frederick

16 (Montgomery County)

Frederick region

Frederick

MC region

I-270

VA-WV border

Plains region

DC

I-66

Nokesville region

6. Some Flat from Frederick

Distance *mi*	45.1
Category	II
Climbing *ft*	2558
Rel. climb *ft/mi*	56.7

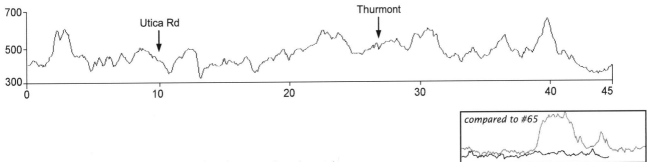

Start   Waverly Elementary School in Frederick, Md.

Route   The first ten miles of this ride reverse the closing ten miles of CATOCTIN CLIMBER (#7) and feature generally small rolling hills through the outlying suburbs of Frederick. At Utica Road, the routes part ways. The next seventeen miles to Thurmont do not result in much elevation change, although the feel of the roads might be otherwise: gradual climbs with steeper descents. After Thurmont, the ride crosses route 15 three times before winding back to Frederick.

Notes   We associate Frederick with difficult hills because the first ride we did from Frederick was CATOCTIN CLIMBER. Adding AROUND ANTIETAM (#8) to the region's ride list only cemented this impression in our minds. In marked contrast, this ride is relatively flat and stays east of the Catoctin Mountains and Route 15. It also takes you over three of the area's historic covered bridges. The third such bridge was the site for the cover picture from *Chuck and Gail's Favorite Bike Rides*, the cycling guide that provided the original inspiration for this book. Just past that bridge on the right is a nice little park—take a break and enjoy the scenery!

7. Catoctin Climber

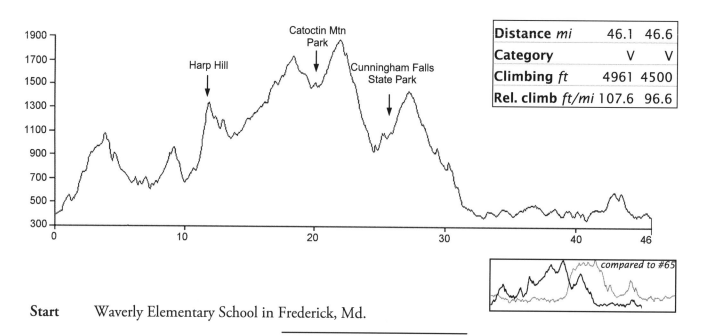

Distance *mi*	46.1	46.6
Category	V	V
Climbing *ft*	4961	4500
Rel. climb *ft/mi*	107.6	96.6

compared to #65

Start   Waverly Elementary School in Frederick, Md.

Route   Depending on the route, this ride varies from extremely hard to difficult. The classic 46-mile route (profiled above) has three big climbs: Harp Hill, Catoctin Mountain Park, and Cunningham Falls State Park. The slightly longer 47-mile route skips the two latter climbs, and if you stay on Wolfsville Road to avoid Harp Hill, you skip all three climbs, climbing only 4252 feet. The route out of Frederick is uphill for several miles along Route 40 and provides an early test for your legs.

Notes   Portions of Catoctin Mountain Park may be closed on occasion, which prohibits using the short route. We learned this the hard way one time when we approached the entrance to the park only to be stopped by heavily armed Federal agents with a low tolerance for cyclists and no sense of humor! Apparently the mountain provides a good view of Camp David, and when the President of the United States decides to spend a weekend there, all access is foreclosed. For information on park closings, see http://www.nps.gov/cato/pphtml/news.html.

Otherwise, this is a classic late season ride when your climbing legs are in great shape and you want a true challenge. Harp Hill is short but very steep, most cruelly in the last stair-step section just before the summit. Sadly, Jim at times has been reduced to weaving across the entire width of the road to make the top, while Scott sits and spins steadily up the climb! The descent off Catoctin Mountain Park is fast and furious thanks to the smooth as glass pavement. The longer descent once you pass Cunningham Falls is entirely different—winding around corners, across one-lane bridges, and generally demanding your full attention. Finish this ride and you will experience a great sense of accomplishment to go along with your aching legs!

A Chuck & Gail ride.

8. Around Antietam

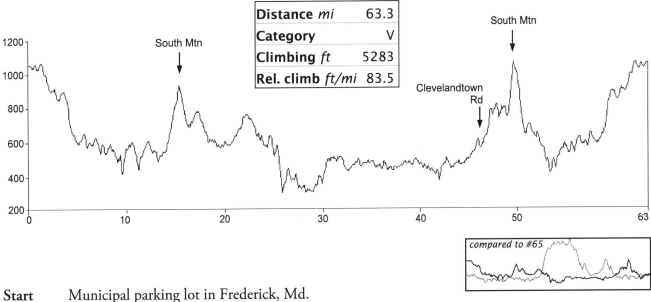

Distance *mi*	63.3
Category	V
Climbing *ft*	5283
Rel. climb *ft/mi*	83.5

compared to #65

Start Municipal parking lot in Frederick, Md.

Route This ride opens easy, with the first ten miles dropping 700 feet of elevation. The first climb of South Mountain begins at about mile fifteen. As hard as it may look on the profile, this climb barely makes the top five on this ride. As you turn north towards Sharpsburg, the ride moves through heavily wooded roads with almost no cars. Route 65 north of Sharpsburg is entirely different, but once you turn off onto Taylors Landing Road the traffic mostly subsides again. The stretch from Sharpsburg to Boonsboro is much flatter than the rest of the ride—let your legs recover if you can, because three hard climbs come soon: Clevelandtown Road in Boonsboro, followed very shortly by the second climb of South Mountain, then Cherry Lane back to the ridge.

Notes This is a very tough ride, perhaps our toughest. The ride crosses South Mountain twice: once on the southern shoulder by Burkittsville and once on Reno Monument Road. Several other challenging climbs are scattered throughout, particularly the "brown cliff" climb of Clevelandtown Road. At the end of the ride, the climb back up Cherry Lane will finish off your legs if they have anything left. Enjoy!

6. Some Flat from Frederick

Distance:	45 miles	
Rating:	II	
Start:	Waverly Elementary School in Frederick, Md.	

0.0	L	Waverly Dr from school
0.2	L	Shookstown Rd at T
0.6	R	Kemp Lane
1.8	L	Rocky Springs Rd at T
3.2	BR	Rocky Springs Rd at Indian Springs Rd
3.7	S	Walter Martz Rd
4.6	L	Christopher's Crossing
4.8	L	Walter Martz at Poole Jones Rd
5.7	L	Oppossumtown Pike
5.9	BR	TRO Opp'twn Pk at Ford Rd
6.5	BL	TRO Opp'twn at Sunday Ln
6.7	R	Masser Rd
8.4	R	Mountaindale Rd
8.8	L	Hansonville Rd (unmarked)
9.0	X	US 15 & L on Hessong Bridge Rd
10.1	R	Utica Rd over covered bridge
11.0	L	Old Frederick Rd
15.0	BL	Creagersville Rd at SS
15.3	R	Old Frederick Rd
21.3	L	Motter's Station Rd (unmarked) - 4th paved rd after covered bridge
21.9	L	Old Kiln Rd (unmarked)
24.4	L	Roddy Rd at T
26.0	S	Apple Church Rd
26.4	R	77, East Main St (unmarked) in **Thurmont**
27.1	L	806, Water St
27.2	R	806, Frederick Rd. B/c Catoctin Furnace Rd
31.1	S	Auburn Rd, crossing US-15
33.1	L	Angleburger Rd, crossing US-15
33.6	R	Hessong Bridge Rd
34.0	R	Fish Hatchery Rd
34.9	L	Bethel Rd
39.7	L	Yellow Springs Rd. B/c Rosemont Ave
43.5	R	Montevue Lane
44.1	BR	Shookstown Rd
44.9	L	Waverly Dr
45.1	R	into school

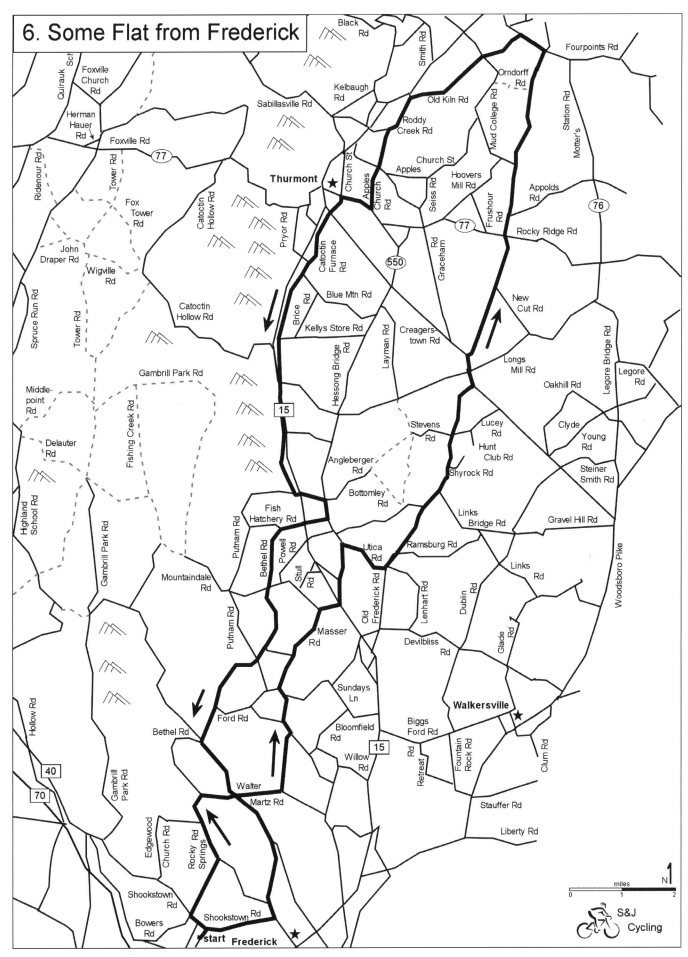

6. Some Flat from Frederick

Black Rd
Smith Rd
Fourpoints Rd
Quirauk Sch
Foxville Church Rd
Kelbaugh Rd
Orndorff Rd
Old Kiln Rd
Herman Hauer Rd
Sabillasville Rd
Roddy Creek Rd
Mud College Rd
Station Rd
Motter's
Foxville Rd
77
Ridenour Rd
Tower Rd
Church St
Apples
Church St
Hoovers Mill Rd
Appolds Rd
76
Fox Tower Rd
Thurmont
Apples Church Rd
Seiss Rd
Frushour Rd
Catoctin Hollow Rd
Pryor Rd
77
Rocky Ridge Rd
John Draper Rd
Wigville Rd
Catoctin Furnace Rd
Brice Rd
Blue Mtn Rd
550
Graceham Rd
New Cut Rd
Catoctin Hollow Rd
Kellys Store Rd
Creagerstown Rd
Longs Mill Rd
Legore Bridge Rd
Spruce Run Rd
Hessong Bridge Rd
Layman Rd
Legore Rd
Gambrill Park Rd
Tower Rd
15
Oakhill Rd
Middlepoint Rd
Fishing Creek Rd
Stevens Rd
Lucey Rd
Clyde
Young Rd
Delauter Rd
Angleberger Rd
Hunt Club Rd
Shyrock Rd
Steiner Smith Rd
Highland School Rd
Bottomley Rd
Links Bridge Rd
Gravel Hill Rd
Fish Hatchery Rd
Putnam Rd
Ramsburg Rd
Links Rd
Gambrill Park Rd
Mountaindale Rd
Bethel Rd
Powell Rd
Stull Rd
Utica Rd
Old Frederick Rd
Lenhart Rd
Dublin Rd
Woodsboro Pike
Putnam Rd
Masser Rd
Glade Rd
Hollow Rd
Ford Rd
Sundays Ln
Devilbliss Rd
Walkersville
Clum Rd
40
Bethel Rd
Bloomfield Rd
Biggs Ford Rd
Retreat Rd
Fountain Rock Rd
70
Walter Martz Rd
Willow Rd
15
Edgewood Church Rd
Gambrill Park Rd
Rocky Rd Springs
Stauffer Rd
Shookstown Rd
Liberty Rd
Bowers Rd
Shookstown Rd
start Frederick

miles
0 1 2
N

S&J Cycling

33

7. Catoctin Climber

Distance: **46** or 47 miles
Rating: V
Start: Waverly Elementary School in Frederick, Md.

46 Mile Ride

0.0	L	Waverly Dr from school
0.2	L	Shookstown Rd at T
0.6	L	Bowers Rd
1.6	R	Rte 40 at T
5.1	L	Hollow Rd at Rosebud Ct on downhill then
5.1	R	Hollow Rd at SS (X rt 40 at 6.3)
7.4	R	Harmony Rd
10.1	R	Wolfsville Rd at T then
10.1	BL	Harp Hill Rd
13.4	BL	17, Wolfsville Rd in **Wolfsville**
13.5	R	Stottlemeyer Rd (store)
13.7	L	Brandenburg Hollow Rd
16.5	R	Garfield Rd at T
17.2	L	Stottlemeyer Rd at T; b/c Foxville-Deerfield Rd at 77
20.1 ☞*	BR	Foxville-Deerfield Rd at Herman Hauver Rd
20.2	BR	Manahan Rd into park
21.0	R	Park Central Rd at SS
24.7	R	77, Foxville Rd at T
24.9	L	Catoctin Hollow Rd
31.4	R	15 ☹

32.1	L	806
32.4	R	Blacks Mill Rd
33.6 ☞*	R	Hessong Bridge Rd
35.1	S	Hessong Bridge Rd at SS at Angleberger Rd
37.0	S	Hansonville Rd at 15 (store)
37.1	R	Mountaindale Rd
37.5	L	Masser Rd
39.2	L	Oppossumtown Pk at T
39.4	R	Opp'twn Pk at Sunday Ln
40.0	BL	TRO Opp'twn Pk at Ford Rd
40.2	R	Walter Martz Rd
41.3	R	Christopher's Crossing at Poole Jones Rd
41.5	BR	Walter Martz Rd
42.3	S	Rocky Springs Rd to cross Yellow Springs Rd
42.9	L	Rocky Springs Rd at Indian Springs Rd
44.4	R	Kemps Ln
45.6	L	Shookstown Rd at SS
45.9	R	Waverly Dr
46.1	R	into school

*47 Mile Ride

20.2	BL	TRO Foxville-Deerfield Rd
20.7	BR	TRO Foxville-Deerfield Rd at Foxville Church Ed
24.3	R	550 at T. B/c Church Rd in **Thurmont**. B/c 806

29.3	R	Frederick St at Park La & Water St
29.7	L	Moser Rd
31.4	R	Hessong Bridge Rd. Rejoin 46 mi route in 4.2 mi at 35.1 turn

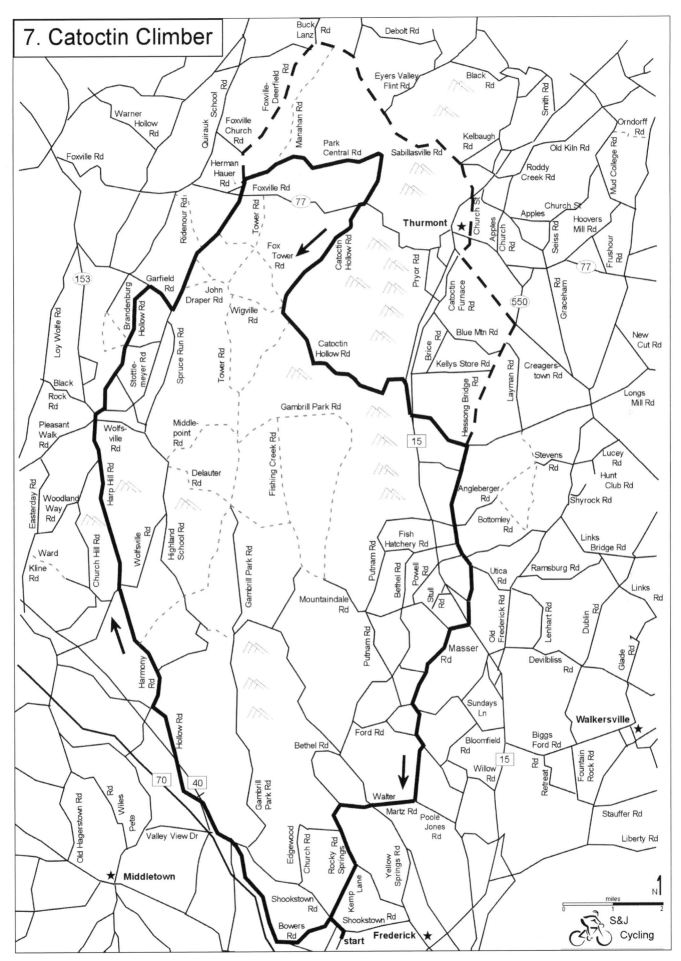

7. Catoctin Climber

Buck Lanz Rd
Debolt Rd
Foxville-Deerfield Rd
Eyers Valley Flint Rd
Black Rd
Smith Rd
Orndorff Rd
Warner Hollow Rd
Quirauk School Rd
Foxville Church Rd
Manahan Rd
Park Central Rd
Sabillasville Rd
Kelbaugh Rd
Old Kiln Rd
Mud College Rd
Foxville Rd
Herman Hauer Rd
Foxville Rd
77
Roddy Creek Rd
Church St
Apples Church St
Hoovers Mill Rd
Ridenour Rd
Tower Rd
Fox Tower Rd
Catoctin Hollow Rd
Thurmont
Church St
Apples Church Rd
Seiss Rd
Frushour Rd
77
153
Garfield Rd
Brandenburg Hollow Rd
John Draper Rd
Wigville Rd
Pryor Rd
Catoctin Furnace Rd
550
Grackeham Rd
New Cut Rd
Loy Wolfe Rd
Stottlemeyer Rd
Spruce Run Rd
Tower Rd
Catoctin Hollow Rd
Brice Rd
Blue Mtn Rd
Kellys Store Rd
Creagerstown Rd
Longs Mill Rd
Black Rock Rd
Gambrill Park Rd
Hessong Bridge Rd
Layman Rd
Pleasant Walk Rd
Wolfsville Rd
Middlepoint Rd
15
Stevens Rd
Lucey Rd
Hunt Club Rd
Easterday Rd
Harp Hill Rd
Delauter Rd
Angleberger Rd
Shyrock Rd
Woodland Way Rd
Church Hill Rd
Wolfsville Rd
Highland School Rd
Gambrill Park Rd
Fishing Creek Rd
Bottomley Rd
Links Bridge Rd
Ward Kline Rd
Fish Hatchery Rd
Ramsburg Rd
Links Rd
Putnam Rd
Bethel Rd
Powell Rd
Utica Rd
Lenhart Rd
Dublin Rd
Mountaindale Rd
Stull Rd
Old Frederick Rd
Glade Rd
Harmony Rd
Putnam Rd
Masser Rd
Devilbliss Rd
Walkersville
Hollow Rd
Sundays Ln
Bloomfield Rd
Biggs Ford Rd
15
70
40
Gambrill Park Rd
Ford Rd
Walter
Martz Rd
Willow Rd
Retreat Rd
Fountain Rock Rd
Old Hagerstown Rd
Wiles Rd
Pete Rd
Valley View Dr
Edgewood
Church Rd
Rocky Springs Rd
Poole Jones Rd
Stauffer Rd
Middletown
Bethel Rd
Kemp Lane
Yellow Springs Rd
Liberty Rd
Shookstown Rd
Bowers Rd
Shookstown Rd
start
Frederick

S&J Cycling

miles
0   1   2

N

8. Around Antietam

Distance:	63 miles	
Rating:	V	
Start:	Municipal parking lot in Frederick, Md.	

0.0	R	40 westbound
0.6	L	Ridge Rd
2.7	L	then R at SL to Maryland Av
3.1	R	Jefferson Blvd at SS
4.1	R	Cherry Ln at SS (Clifton Rd on L)
5.2	R	Holter Rd at SS
8.9	R	Church St in **Middletown**
9.1	L	Main St (stores)
9.4	L	Walnut St, b/c Bidle Rd
11.0	L	Picnic Woods Rd at SS
13.5	R	Arnoldstown Rd at SS, b/c Gapland Rd
15.7	R	at top of hill, then R on Townsend Rd
17.0	R	67, Rohrersville Rd
17.5	L	Trego Rd
19.4	L	Chestnut Grove Rd
24.7	R	Harpers Ferry Rd at T
25.8	L	Limekiln Rd on downhill
28.3	S	Harpers Ferry Rd at SS in **Antietam Village**
28.5	L	Canal Rd
30.0	R	Millers Saw Mill
31.7	L	Harpers Ferry Rd at T
32.5	R	34, E Main St in **Sharpsburg**
32.7	L	65, N Church St, b/c Sharpsburg Pike
35.8	L	Taylors Landing Rd
36.2	R	Fairplay Rd
38.7	BR	63 at SS in **Fairplay**
39.1	S	Manor Church Rd at 65
42.5	L	Wheeler Rd at T
42.6	BR	Monroe Rd at Y
44.3	L	34 at T ☹
45.3	R	Alt 40 in **Boonsboro**
46.7	R	Clevelandtown Rd
47.0	L	Reno Monument Rd at SS
50.5	BR	Bolivar Rd at SS
51.3	BL	Marker Rd
53.1	R	Alt 40
54.2	R	Church St
54.4	L	Franklin St, b/c Holter Rd
58.1	L	Cherry Ln
59.1	L	Jefferson Blvd
59.8	L	Maryland Ave
60.5	L	then quick R to Ridge Rd
62.7	R	40
63.3	R	to parking lot

8. Around Antietam

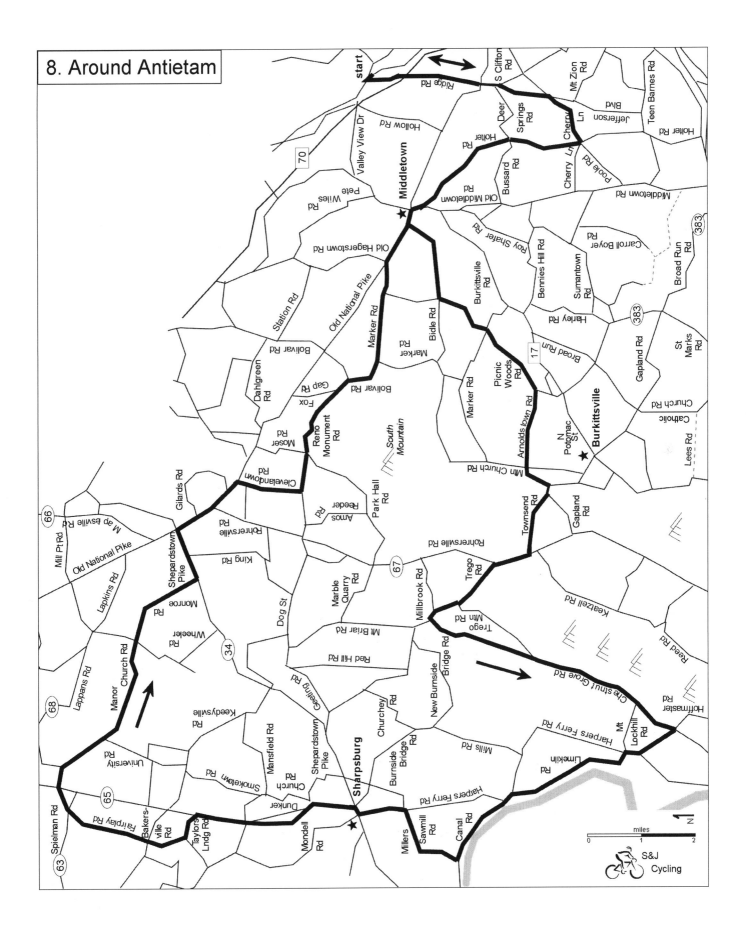

Montgomery County region

Bounded by the Potomac River to the south and I-270 to the east, all rides head north (or west) from Riley's Lock or Poolesville. Riley's Lock is our start point closest to D.C., but it does not feel that way. The southwest corner of the region—south of Whites Ferry Road and west of Poolesville is amazing—good pavement, few cars, and gorgeous scenery.

Montgomery County also provides a nice intermediate difficulty area—hillier than the Nokesville region but not as hilly as the Marshall rides—with a wide range of distances, mostly in category II and III.

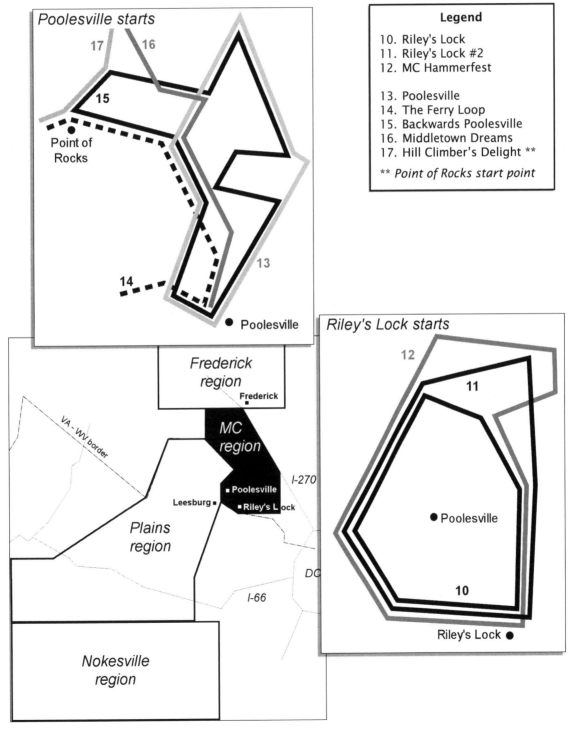

10. Riley's Lock

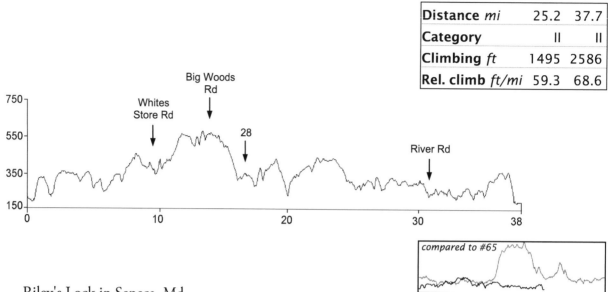

Distance *mi*	25.2	37.7
Category	II	II
Climbing *ft*	1495	2586
Rel. climb *ft/mi*	59.3	68.6

Start   Riley's Lock in Seneca, Md.

Route   After a very brief warm-up riding back to River Road from the parking lot, you face the short but ugly climb at mile 1. Nobody in our group—not even the climbers—likes this climb. It's just too early in the ride. Staying on River Road is no better—you have to gain the elevation either way. Happily, the rest of this ride is pure bliss. The next several roads are gorgeous and have very little traffic. Be careful not to blow the turn onto Old Bucklodge Lane—it's on a slight downhill and appears without much warning. The short route departs a few miles later, making a beeline through Poolesville to River Road. On the long route, Dickerson Road has enough traffic that you should stay single file. After passing by the power plant on Martinsburg Road, the long route takes in the southwest corner of the county, one of the nicest riding areas anywhere.

Notes   Still a classic after all of these years—easy to get to and light traffic. Big Woods Road is fun (the profile shows why) as is the Mt. Nebo Road stretch leading to River Road. Traffic is fairly light throughout. You will be amazed at how portions of this ride make you forget just how close to a major metropolitan area you are.

Sugarland Road and Martinsburg Road feature the two instances of "old style" pavement (a concrete center with dirt/gravel sides) that we know of in Montgomery County. Although trickier to ride when cars are present, these roads make the ride feel all the more rural.

A Chuck & Gail ride.

11. Riley's Lock #2

Distance *mi*	43.2
Category	III
Climbing *ft*	2900
Rel. climb *ft/mi*	67.1

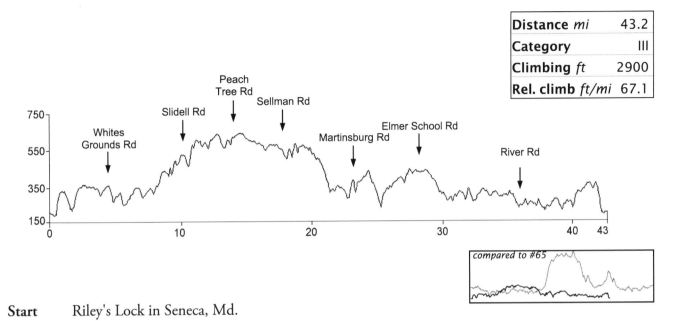

Start   Riley's Lock in Seneca, Md.

Route   The ride is RILEY'S LOCK (#10) with miles 7 to 18 added in place of a 6-mile stretch of the original. Like all Riley's Lock rides, this ride opens with that painful climb at mile 1. Barnesville Road has several decent climbs that are possible to take at speed—if you're in shape. After the turn onto Slidell Road, the first climb has a second stair step hidden around a bend—good to know if your group plays "king of the mountain" like ours often does. After rejoining the original Riley's Lock course, the mile-and-a-half on Bealesville Road has a challenging triple climb—plenty of time for chasers to catch you if you attack early and fade.

Notes   We designed this ride back when we had a dearth of Montgomery County rides—only POOLESVILLE (35 miles) and RILEY'S LOCK (38 miles)—and have liked it since our first ride. Bounded as it is by the Potomac and I-270, Riley's Lock is limited in the number of rides it offers, but the three main rides we feature here are enough to make it one of our favorite start points.

Barnesville Road brings with it a couple of small climbs, but save a little something for the opening climb on Slidell Road. Jim has loved Slidell Road since his first mile on it, while Scott favors Peach Tree Road southbound. The course is generally rolling throughout with a fun downhill blast on Mt. Nebo Road prior to the finishing stretch on River Road. The pavement on Mt. Nebo has been rough for some years, so be careful on the descent.

12. MC Hammerfest

Distance *mi*	47.3	51.4
Category	III	III
Climbing *ft*	3332	3600
Rel. climb *ft/mi*	70.4	70.0

Start   Riley's Lock in Seneca, Md.

Route   The opening twenty miles reverse the original RILEY'S LOCK ride to good effect. Once at the base of Sugarloaf, the route heads east on Comus Road (another favorite of Jim's) a bit farther than any of our other rides. The turn onto Shiloh Church Road is at the base of hill, and although you see a road for a while before you reach it, be careful not to go flying by the turn. A few small hills stand in the way before the route connects back to Peach Tree Road. Once on Peach Tree, the rest of the ride is fairly flat, but for the seemingly never-ending rollers of River Road on the long version. One last downhill turn to watch for is the turn back onto Riley's Lock Road, as you give back that elevation you painfully gained in the opening mile.

Notes   The third of our Riley's Lock rides, MC HAMMERFEST gives you fifty gorgeous miles in Montgomery County while staying south of Sugarloaf. The long version traverses most of River Road at the end. We keep thinking we should count the River Road rollers, just so we would know, but decided that perhaps ignorance really is bliss.

Even though this ride is in the heart of our Montgomery County riding area, it still manages to be the only ride to use a fair number of roads, making it feel like a new ride each time.

13. Poolesville

Distance *mi*	24.0	35.2	42.0
Category	II	III	III
Climbing *ft*	1337	2517	2875
Rel. climb *ft/mi*	55.7	71.5	68.5

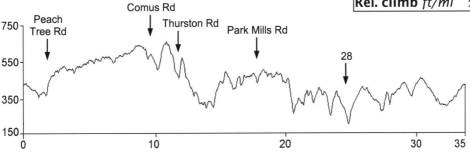

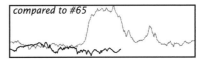

Start   Poolesville High School in Poolesville, Md.

Route   The two longer routes are counterclockwise loops around Sugarloaf Mountain; the short route is also a loop, but one that stays south of the mountain. With the exception of Dickerson Road and the short stretch on Fingerboard Road, this ride suffers very little from traffic. As the profile shows, the jags get a little larger as the miles add up, but none of the later climbs feel hard.

Notes   The 35-mile ride is Chuck & Gail's classic loop around Sugarloaf. Park Mills Road southbound is particularly fun with several quick climbs and swooping descents. The longer route takes out some of the enjoyable Park Mills stretch but adds a little welcome distance. Rolling throughout.

Mostly a Chuck & Gail ride.

14. The Ferry Loop

Distance *mi*	43.9
Category	III
Climbing *ft*	3033
Rel. climb *ft/mi*	69.1

Start   Poolesville High School in Poolesville, Md.

Route   This ride suffers from an alternating split personality—the roads are either gorgeous, low-traffic roads or still nice roads with more traffic. The first seven miles are gorgeous (Poolesville to just beyond the ferry). The next three miles are trafficky (on Route 15 and Business-15 to Leesburg). The following 18 miles are gorgeous, heading north through Virginia until the turn onto Route 15 before crossing back into Maryland). The final fourteen miles are back in the trafficky-but-still-nice category. An alternative finish to this ride turns off Route 28 at the top of the climb past Dickerson and follows the closing miles of POOLESVILLE (#13). It's a trade-off between traffic and road variety.

Notes   This ride is the first of three "bridge" rides that connect two of our regions. This ride bridges The Plains and the Montgomery County, MIDDLETOWN DREAMS (#16) connects Frederick and Montgomery County, and Picnic from THE PLAINS (#45) bridges The Plains and Nokesville.

The section from Waterford to Point of Rocks in Virginia has few equals in terms of quality. We so enjoy that section that we "borrowed" it for LOVETTS OR LEES IT (#40). On the other hand, Business-15 into Leesburg is a heavily trafficked road, although with a good shoulder. Make sure to bring some money to pay for the ferry crossing!

15. Backwards Poolesville

Distance *mi*	50.5
Category	III
Climbing *ft*	3656
Rel. climb *ft/mi*	72.4

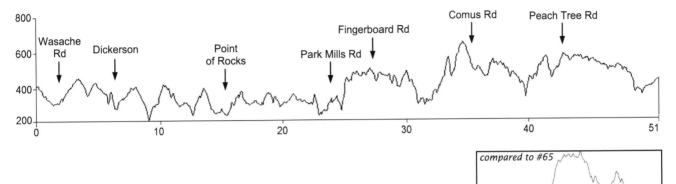

Start   Poolesville High School in Poolesville, Md.

Route   You begin by heading northwest from Poolesville to Point of Rocks on mostly flat roads, but for the climb up to the power plant on Wasache Road. The stretch from Point of Rocks to Sugarloaf is particularly enjoyable, with little traffic and still fairly flat roads. The real fun begins on Park Mills Road, with one steep climb and several smaller ones. The last third of the ride—down the east side of Sugarloaf—is mostly rolling.

Notes   This ride might be the granddaddy of them all—it was the first area route laid out by Chuck back in 1977. The first time we rode this ride, a freak thunderstorm on Peach Tree Road drenched us. We rode into Poolesville dripping wet and found the town totally dry, with not even a hint of rain.

16. Middletown Dreams

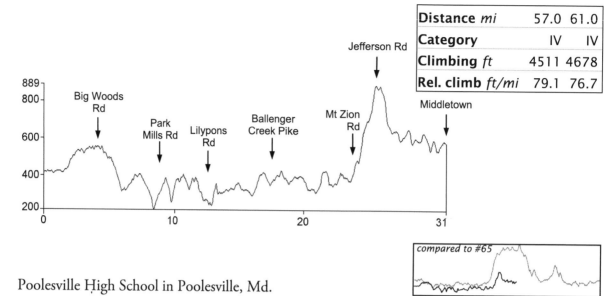

Distance *mi*		57.0	61.0
Category		IV	IV
Climbing *ft*		4511	4678
Rel. climb *ft/mi*		79.1	76.7

Start Poolesville High School in Poolesville, Md.

Route The first half of the ride is fairly flat, skirting south around Sugarloaf Mountain and running along the flat plain to its northwest. Then the fun begins: Mt. Zion Road has several good climbs northbound and Holter Road seems to be all uphill rollers no matter which direction you are riding. Jefferson Road runs along a small ridge and once you climb it you immediately drop off the other side on the run into the halfway point in Middletown.

Notes This ride bridges two of our riding areas: Montgomery County and Frederick. It is also our only out-and-back route, making it easy to make the ride whatever distance you would like. For example, if your legs are not up to the tough climb up to Jefferson Road, do the ride to Mt. Zion and back. We generally prefer loop rides, preferring changing scenery, but out-and-back rides have the advantage of having pre-written cues for reversing.

17. Hill Climber's Delight

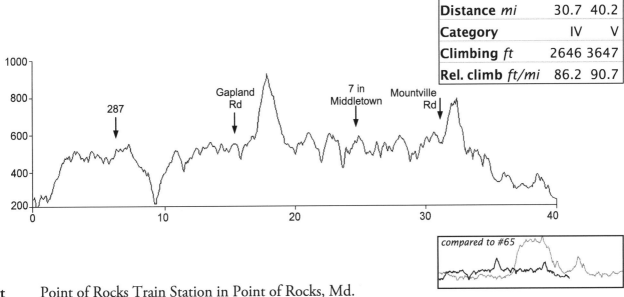

Distance *mi*	30.7	40.2
Category	IV	V
Climbing *ft*	2646	3647
Rel. climb *ft/mi*	86.2	90.7

compared to #65

Start Point of Rocks Train Station in Point of Rocks, Md.

Route After crossing the Potomac into Virginia, you face the first climb up from the river. Like real estate, hills are all about location, and this climb is harder because it comes so early in the ride. The road to Lovettsville is fairly flat. All too soon, you lose that hard-won elevation as you descend to the Potomac. The second climb is again one up from the shores of the Potomac. After another relatively flat stretch, the third and hardest climb is up the shoulder of South Mountain. The roads to the final climb on Mountville Road are not quite as flat as the previous ones, but the roads are generally downhill from the top of the climb back to Point of Rocks.

Notes This is a deceptive ride. The first two climbs, at miles 1.3 and 9.3, don't push the 40-mile ride into category V. It's not until the far side of Burkittsville that the climb to South Mountain begins. Since this is at mile 17 and the climb ends at mile 18, it prompted the now classic comment from Scott, "It's only a mile until the top of the climb—how bad can it be?" Bad. Several small hills lead to the fourth climb on Mountville Road. Overall, this is a short but challenging ride.

A Chuck & Gail ride.

10. Riley's Lock

Distance:	25 or **38** miles
Rating:	II
Start:	Riley's Lock in Seneca, Md.

38 Mile Ride

0.0	R	Riley's Lock Rd from parking	14.5	R	Big Woods Rd
0.7	L	River Rd at T	17.0	L	28, Dickerson Rd at T
0.8	R	Old River Rd	18.2	BR	Martinsburg Rd
1.0	R	Montevideo Rd at T	19.4	BR	Martinsburg Rd at Wasache Rd at Y
3.2	R	Sugarland Rd at Y	22.9	R	Whites Ferry Rd at T
4.8	L	28, Darnestown Rd at T	23.1	L	Elmer School Rd
4.9	R	121, White Grounds Rd	25.2	L	Club Hollow Rd
6.6	BL	White Grounds Rd at Schaeffer Rd	27.2	R	Edwards Ferry Rd at T
7.5	L	Old Bucklodge La	27.3	BR	Edwards Ferry Rd at Westerly Rd
9.5	L	Bucklodge Rd at T	28.7	L	West Offutt Rd
10.1 ☞ *	R	Whites Store Rd	29.5	S	Mt Nebo Rd, b/c River Rd
11.9	R	Peach Tree Rd at T	37.0	R	Riley's Lock Rd
12.4	L	Sellman Rd	37.7	L	into parking lot
13.0	L	109, Beallsville Rd at T			

*25 Mile Ride

11.9	L	Peach Tree Rd at T	17.1	L	Hughes Rd
14.5	L	28, Darnestown Rd at T	20.1	L	Sugarland Rd
14.8	R	Cattail Rd	22.0	R	Partnership Rd
16.7	L	Cattail Rd at SS	23.7	L	River Rd at T
16.8	L	Fisher Ave at T in **Poolesville**	24.5	R	Rileys Lock Rd
16.9	R	Wootton Ave	25.2	L	to parking

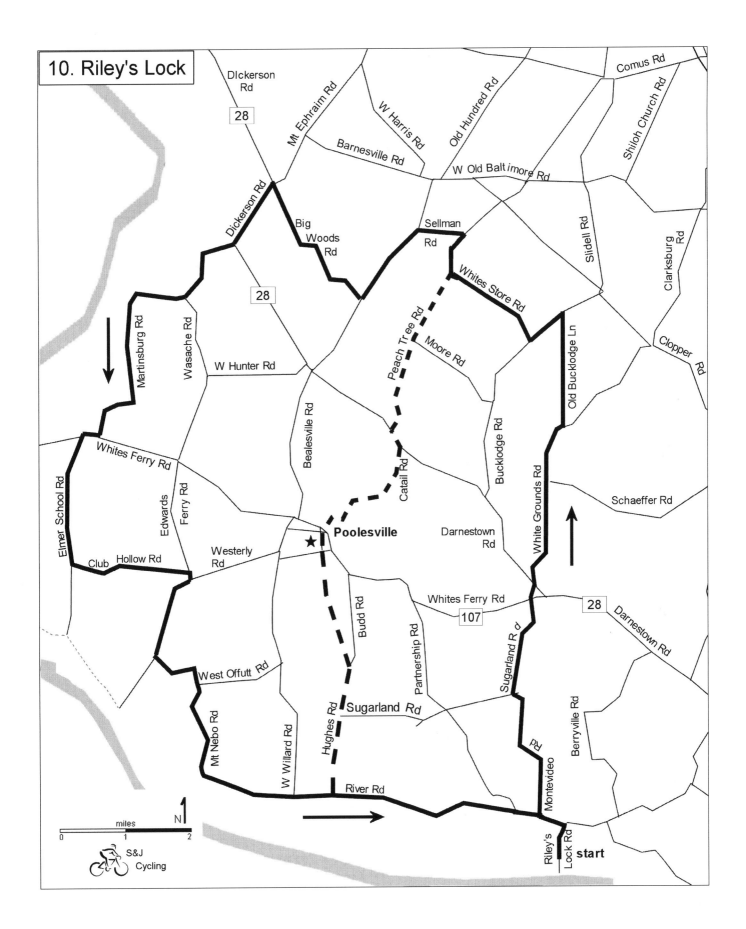

10. Riley's Lock

Dickerson Rd

28

Mt Ephraim Rd

W Harris Rd

Old Hundred Rd

Comus Rd

Barnesville Rd

W Old Baltimore Rd

Shiloh Church Rd

Dickerson Rd

Big Woods Rd

Sellman Rd

Whites Store Rd

Slidell Rd

Clarksburg Rd

28

Martinsburg Rd

Wasache Rd

W Hunter Rd

Peach Tree Rd

Moore Rd

Old Bucklodge Ln

Clopper Rd

Bealesville Rd

Catail Rd

Bucklodge Rd

White Grounds Rd

Schaeffer Rd

Whites Ferry Rd

Poolesville

Darnestown Rd

Elmer School Rd

Edwards Ferry Rd

Club Hollow Rd

Westerly Rd

Whites Ferry Rd

107

Sugarland Rd

28

Darnestown Rd

Budd Rd

Partnership Rd

West Offutt Rd

Sugarland Rd

Mt Nebo Rd

W Willard Rd

Hughes Rd

River Rd

Montevideo Rd

Berryville Rd

miles

0   1   2

N

S&J Cycling

Riley's Lock Rd   **start**

11. Riley's Lock #2

Distance:	43 miles
Rating:	III
Start:	Riley's Lock in Seneca, Md.

0.0	R	Riley's Lock Rd from parking
0.7	L	River Rd at T
1.0	R	Montevideo Rd
3.1	R	Sugarland Rd at Y
4.8	L	28, Darnestown Rd at T
4.9	R	121, White Grounds Rd
6.6	BL	White Grounds Rd at Schaeffer Rd
9.3	R	Clopper Rd
9.4	L	Clarksburg Rd
9.5	L	117, Barnesville Rd. Bear left after underpass
10.6	R	Slidell Rd
14.2	L	95, Comus Rd
14.5	L	Peach Tree Rd
18.0	R	Sellman Rd after bridge
18.5	L	109, Bealesville Rd at T
20.0	R	Big Woods Rd
22.5	L	28, Dickerson Rd at T
23.7	BR	Martinsburg Rd
24.9	BR	Martinsburg Rd at Wasache Rd at Y
28.4	R	White's Ferry Rd at T
28.6	L	Elmer School Rd
30.7	L	Club Hollow Rd
32.7	R	Edwards Ferry Rd at T
32.8	BR	Edwards Ferry Rd at Westerly Rd
34.2	L	West Offutt Rd
35.0	S	Mt Nebo Rd, becomes River Rd
42.5	R	Riley's Lock Rd
43.2	L	into parking lot

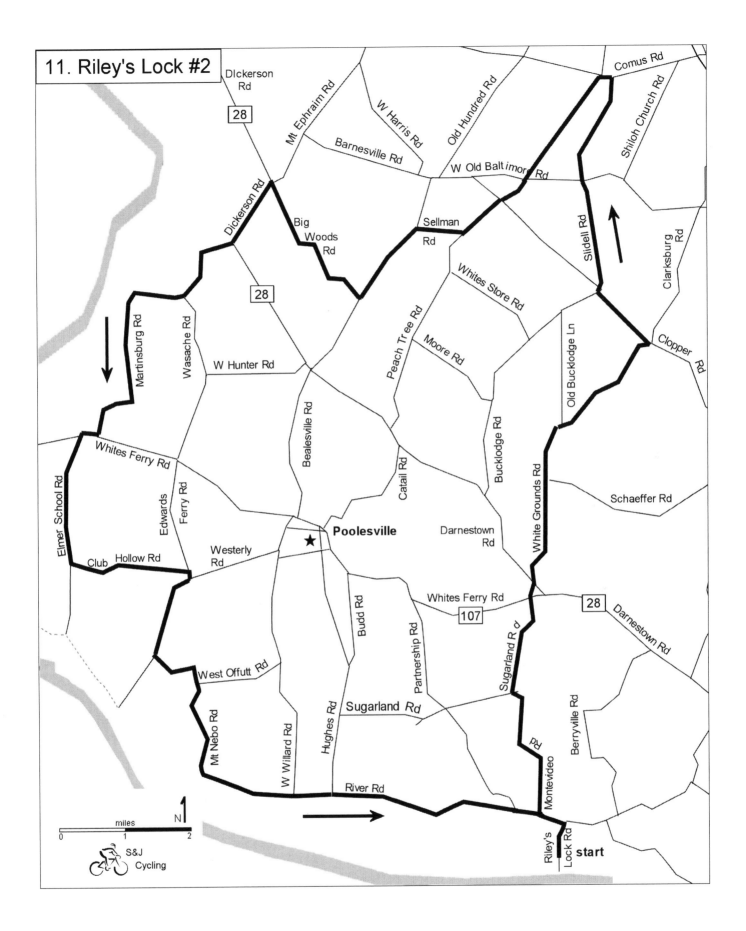

11. Riley's Lock #2

Dickerson Rd

28

Comus Rd

Shiloh Church Rd

Mt Ephraim Rd

W Harris Rd

Old Hundred Rd

Barnesville Rd

W Old Baltimore Rd

Dickerson Rd

Big Woods Rd

Sellman Rd

Slidell Rd

Clarksburg Rd

28

Whites Store Rd

Martinsburg Rd

Wasache Rd

W Hunter Rd

Peach Tree Rd

Moore Rd

Old Bucklodge Ln

Clopper Rd

Bealesville Rd

Bucklodge Rd

White Grounds Rd

Whites Ferry Rd

Schaeffer Rd

Elmer School Rd

Edwards Ferry Rd

Catail Rd

Poolesville

Darnestown Rd

Club Hollow Rd

Westerly Rd

Whites Ferry Rd

107

28

Darnestown Rd

West Offutt Rd

Budd Rd

Partnership Rd

Sugarland Rd

Berryville Rd

Mt Nebo Rd

W Willard Rd

Hughes Rd

Sugarland Rd

Montevideo Rd

miles

N

0   1   2

S&J Cycling

River Rd

Riley's Lock Rd **start**

12. MC Hammerfest

> **Distance:** 47 or 51 miles
> **Rating:** III
> **Start:** Riley's Lock in Seneca, Md.

47 Mile Ride

0.0	R	Riley's Lock Rd from parking	30.4	R	West Old Baltimore Rd at T
0.7	L	River Rd at T	32.0	L	Peach Tree Rd at T
5.0	S	Mt Nebo Rd	33.9	L	Whites Store Rd
8.1	S	West Offutt Rd	35.8	L	Bucklodge Rd at T
9.0	R	Edward's Ferry Rd at T	36.4	R	Old Bucklodge Rd
10.3	BL	TRO Edwards Ferry	38.4	R	White Grounds Rd at T
10.4	L	Club Hollow	39.3	BR	TRO White Grounds Rd
12.4	R	Elmer School Rd	41.0	L	Rt 28
14.5	R	Whites Ferry Rd at T	41.1	R	Sugarland Rd
14.7	L	Martinsburg Rd	41.2	X	107, Whites Ferry Rd ☞ *
18.1	BL	TRO Martinsburg Rd	43.9	L	Partnership Rd at SS
19.4	L	Rt 28	45.9	L	River Rd
20.6	R	Mt Ephraim Rd	46.6	R	Riley's Lock Rd
23.4	R	Comus Rd (store at mi 26.0)	47.3	L	into parking lot
28.4	R	Shiloh Church Rd			

*51 Mile Ride

43.9	X	Partnership Rd	46.9	L	River Rd
44.6	R	TRO Sugarland Rd	50.7	R	Riley's Lock Rd
45.8	L	Hughes Rd	51.4	L	into parking lot

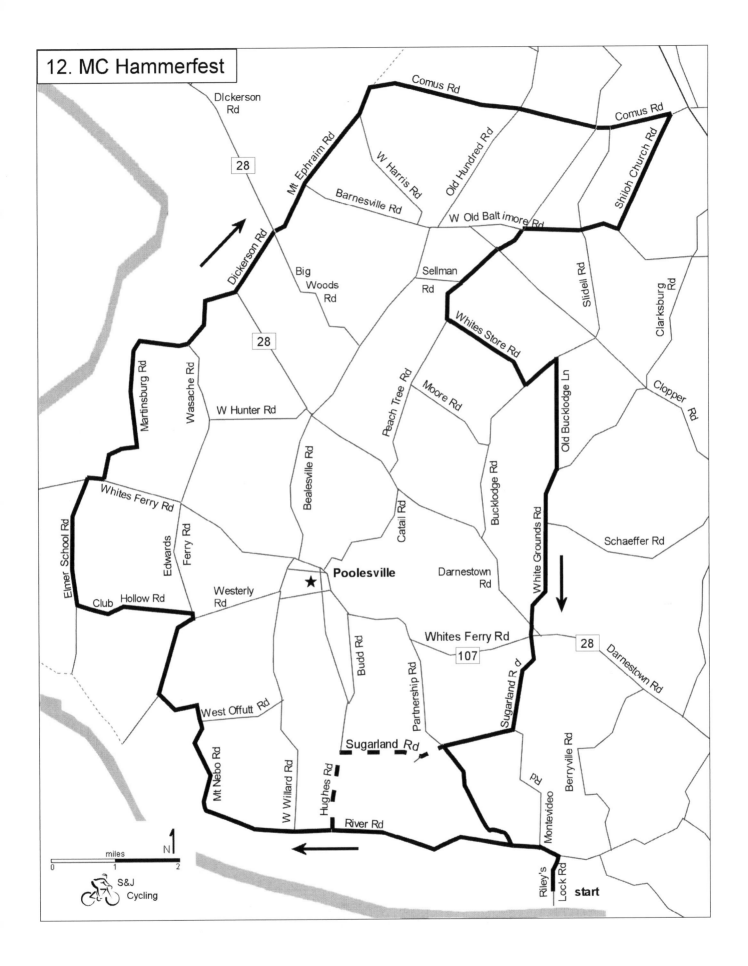

12. MC Hammerfest

13. Poolesville

Distance:	24, **35** or 42 miles
Rating:	II or III
Start:	Poolesville High School in Poolesville, Md.

35 Mile Ride (III)

0.0	R	West Willard Rd		12.4	L	Thurston Rd on downhill
0.1	R	Wooton Ave		17.5	L	Fingerboard Rd at Y
0.7	L	107, Fisher Ave at SS		☞ *		
0.8	R	Cattail Rd		18.8	L	Park Mills Rd
0.9	R	Cattail Rd at T		☞ *		
2.8	L	28, Darnestown Rd at T		25.5	L	28, Dickerson Rd at T (store in **Dickerson**)
3.1	R	Peach Tree Rd		☞ **		
6.2	S	Peach Tree Rd at Selman Rd, crossing bridge		28.9	R	Martinsburg Rd
				30.2	L	Wasche Rd at Y
9.9	L	Comus Rd at SS		32.9	L	Whites Ferry Rd., becomes Fisher Ave
☞ **				35.0	R	West Willard Rd
11.2	R	109, Old Hundred Rd		35.2	L	to parking

*42 Mile Ride (III)

18.8	S	Fingerboard Rd		26.6	R	New Design Rd at SS
20.8	R	Michael's Mill Rd, b/c Manor Woods Rd		26.7	L	Oland Rd, becomes Lilypons Rd
23.2	L	New Design Rd		29.1	R	Park Mills Rd at T. Rejoin 35-mile ride in 3.1 miles
24.6	R	Adamstown Rd				
25.4	L	Mountville Rd at T				

**24 Mile Ride (II)

11.2	S	Comus Rd		16.5	L	28, Dickerson Rd at T. Rejoin 35-mile ride in 1.2 miles at mile 28.9
13.7	BL	Mt Ephraim Rd				

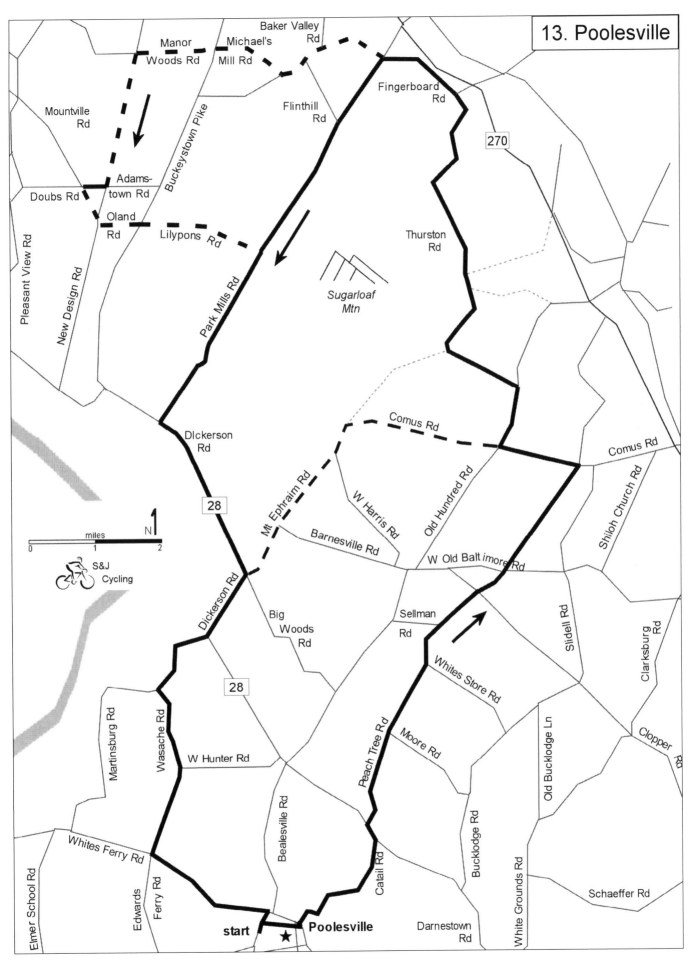

Manor Woods Rd

Baker Valley Rd

Michael's Mill Rd

Mountville Rd

Buckeystown Pike

Flinthill Rd

Fingerboard Rd

270

Adams-town Rd

Doubs Rd

Oland Rd

Lilypons Rd

Park Mills Rd

Thurston Rd

Pleasant View Rd

New Design Rd

Sugarloaf Mtn

Dlckerson Rd

Comus Rd

Comus Rd

28

Mt Ephraim Rd

W Harris Rd

Old Hundred Rd

Shiloh Church Rd

N

miles
0   1   2

S&J Cycling

Barnesville Rd

W Old Balt imore Rd

Slidell Rd

Clarksburg Rd

Dickerson Rd

Big Woods Rd

Sellman Rd

Whites Store Rd

28

Martinsburg Rd

Wasache Rd

W Hunter Rd

Peach Tree Rd

Moore Rd

Old Bucklodge Ln

Clopper Rd

Bealesville Rd

Catail Rd

Bucklodge Rd

White Grounds Rd

Schaeffer Rd

Whites Ferry Rd

Elmer School Rd

Edwards Ferry Rd

start

★ **Poolesville**

Darnestown Rd

55

14. The Ferry Loop

Distance:	44 miles	
Rating:	III	
Start:	Poolesville High School in Poolesville, Md.	

0.0	R	West Willard Rd
0.3	L	107, Fishers Ave, becomes Whites Ferry Rd
6.5		cross Potomac on ferry. Head south on 655
7.7	L	US 15 ☹
8.9	S	Business US 15
10.7	R	Cornwall St in **Leesburg**
11.0	L	Ayr St. Go wrong-way for a block
11.1	S	Dry Mill Rd
13.1	BR	Dry Mill Rd
14.9	X	W&OD trail
15.2	R	9, Charles Town Pike, crossing over 7 ☹
16.0	R	662, Clarke's Gap Rd

18.2	S	665, High St in **Waterford**, becomes Loyalty Rd (store)
24.0	L	663, Taylorstown Rd in **Taylorstown**
26.1	R	672, Lovettsville Rd
28.8	L	US 15. Cross into Maryland
29.1	R	28, Tuscarora Rd in **Point of Rocks**
34.0	R	28, Dickerson Rd at SS
41.1	R	109, Beallesville Rd at light in **Beallesville**
43.5	R	107, Fishers Ave at SS in **Poolesville**
43.6	L	West Willard Rd
43.9	L	parking lot

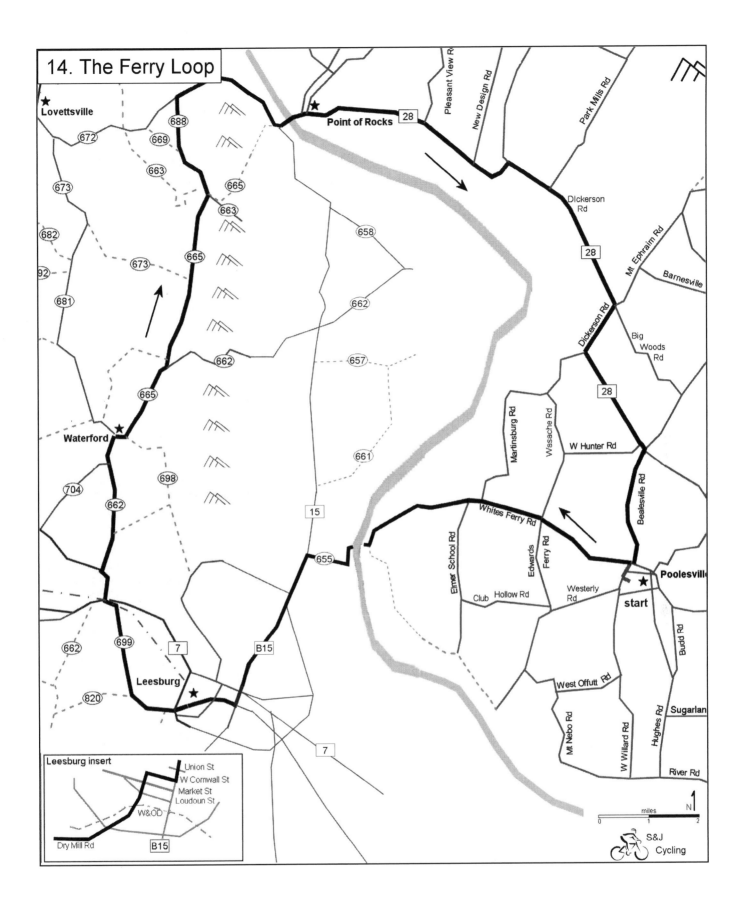

14. The Ferry Loop

Lovettsville

688
672
669
663
673
665
663
682
665
92
673
681
662
665
662
662
657
Waterford
698
661
704
662
15
699
655
662
7
B15
Leesburg
820
7

Point of Rocks
28
Pleasant View Rd
New Design Rd
Park Mills Rd
Dickerson Rd
28
Mt Ephraim Rd
Barnesville
Dickerson Rd
Big Woods Rd
28
Martinsburg Rd
Wasache Rd
W Hunter Rd
Bealesville Rd
Whites Ferry Rd
Elmer School Rd
Edwards Ferry Rd
Club Hollow Rd
Westerly Rd
Poolesville
start
Budd Rd
West Offutt Rd
Sugarlan
Mt Nebo Rd
W Willard Rd
Hughes Rd
River Rd

658
662

Leesburg insert

Union St
W Cornwall St
Market St
Loudoun St
W&OD
Dry Mill Rd
B15

N
miles
0   1   2

S&J Cycling

15. Backwards Poolesville

Distance:	51 miles	
Rating:	III	
Start:	Poolesville High School in Poolesville, Md.	

0.0	R	West Willard Rd (heading north)
0.3	L	107, Fisher's Ave (becomes White's Ferry Rd)
2.4	R	Wasche Rd
5.1	R	Martinsburg Rd
6.4	L	28, Dickerson Rd
7.6	BL	28 after underpass
11.2	L	28 at 85 ☹
15.9	R	Ballenger Creek Rd
19.7	R	Calico Rocks Rd
19.8	BR	Doubs Rd
20.2	L	Doubs Rd after RR tracks at SS
21.1	R	Mountville Rd
21.6	R	New Design Rd
21.7	L	Orland Rd
22.4	S	Lilypons Rd
24.3	L	Park Mills Rd at T
27.8	R	Fingerboard Rd
29.1	R	Thurston Rd
33.0	BL	Thurston Rd at Sugarloaf Rd
34.2	R	109, Old Hundred Rd at T
35.4	R	Comus Rd in **Comus**
37.7	L	Mount Ephraim Rd (leftmost road in parking lot)
39.8	L	Barnesville Rd
43.2	R	Peach Tree Rd
44.3	S	Peach Tree Rd at Sellman Rd
47.5	L	28, Darnestown Rd
47.7	R	Cattail Rd
49.6	L	Cattail Rd at SS
49.8	L	107, Fisher Ave
49.9	R	Wooton Ave
50.5	L	into Poolesville H.S.

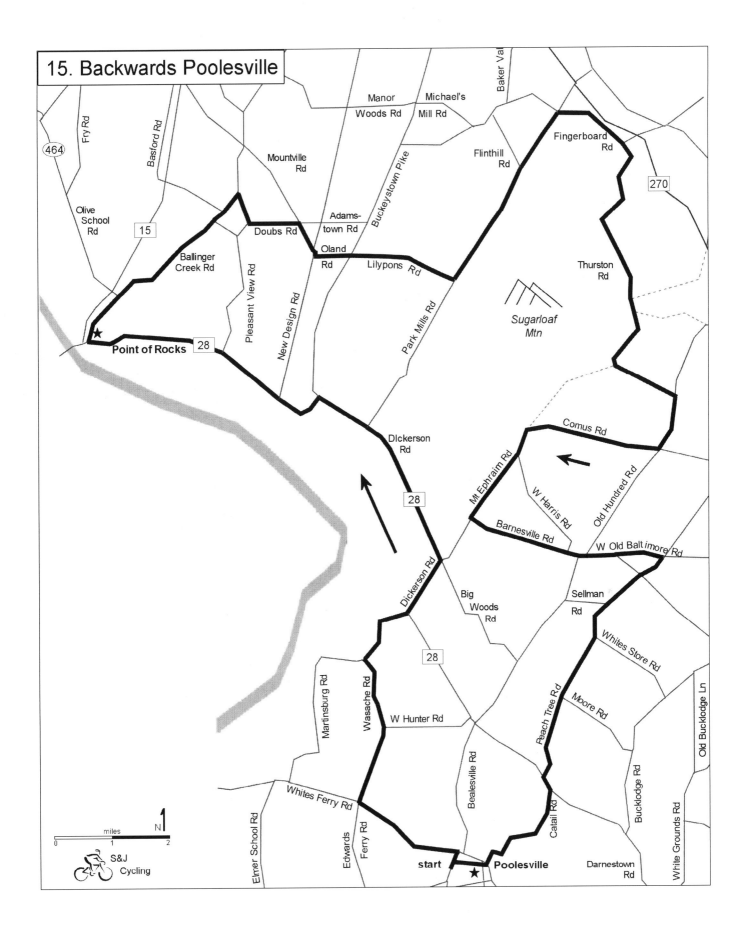

15. Backwards Poolesville

Manor Woods Rd

Michael's Mill Rd

Baker Va

464

Fry Rd

Basford Rd

Mountville Rd

Buckeystown Pike

Flinthill Rd

Fingerboard Rd

270

Olive School Rd

15

Adams-town Rd

Doubs Rd

Oland Rd

Lilypons Rd

Thurston Rd

Ballinger Creek Rd

Pleasant View Rd

New Design Rd

Park Mills Rd

Sugarloaf Mtn

★
Point of Rocks 28

Dickerson Rd

Comus Rd

Mt Ephraim Rd

W Harris Rd

Old Hundred Rd

28

Barnesville Rd

W Old Baltimore Rd

Dickerson Rd

Big Woods Rd

Sellman Rd

Whites Store Rd

28

Martinsburg Rd

Wasache Rd

W Hunter Rd

Peach Tree Rd

Moore Rd

Bucklodge Rd

Old Bucklodge Ln

miles
0   1   2

N

S&J Cycling

Elmer School Rd

Whites Ferry Rd

Edwards Ferry Rd

Bealesville Rd

Catail Rd

start ★ Poolesville

Darnestown Rd

White Grounds Rd

16. Middletown Dreams

Distance:	57 or **61** miles
Rating:	IV
Start:	Poolesville High School in Poolesville, Md.

61 Mile Ride

0.0	R	West Willard Rd
0.3	R	107, Fisher Ave
0.4	L	109, Elgin Rd
0.8	BL	Beallesville Rd
4.1	L	Big Woods Rd
6.7	R	28, Dickerson Rd at T
8.9	R	Park Mills Rd
12.0	L	Lilypons Rd, b/c Oland Rd
14.6	R	New Design Rd at T
14.7	L	Mountville Rd
16.8	R	351, Ballenger Creek Pike
☜*		
20.8	L	Elmer Derr Rd
22.9	R	Cap Stine Rd to cross 15/340
☞*		
23.4	S	Mt Zion Rd at light
25.4	R	Jefferson Blvd
25.8	L	Cherry Lane
26.9	R	Holter Rd, b/c Franklin Rd
30.6		turn around at S Church St at T in **Middletown** (store)

34.3	L	Cherry Lane
35.3	R	Jefferson Blvd at SS
35.7	L	Mt Zion Rd, b/c Cap Stine Rd
☞**		
38.2	L	Elmer Derr Rd after 15/340
40.3	R	351, Ballenger Crk Pk at SS
☞**		
44.3	L	Mountville Rd
46.4	R	New Design Rd at SS
46.5	L	Oland Rd, b/c Lilypons Rd
49.1	R	Park Mills Rd at T
52.2	L	28, Dickerson Rd at T
54.4	L	Big Woods Rd
56.9	R	109, Beallesville Rd at T
60.7	R	107, Fisher Ave
60.8	L	West Willard Rd
61.0	L	into Poolesville H.S.

*57 Mile Ride, part 1

19.8	L	South Renn Rd
20.3	R	Cap Stine Rd, cross 15/340 at mile 21.1
☜*		back to main ride

**57 Mile Ride, part 2

38.2	S	Cap Stine Rd after crossing 15/340
39.0	L	South Renn Rd
39.5	R	351, Ballenger Creek Pike

16. Middletown Dreams

Map 1: Poolesville - Lilypons Rd

Map 2: Lilypons Rd - Middletown

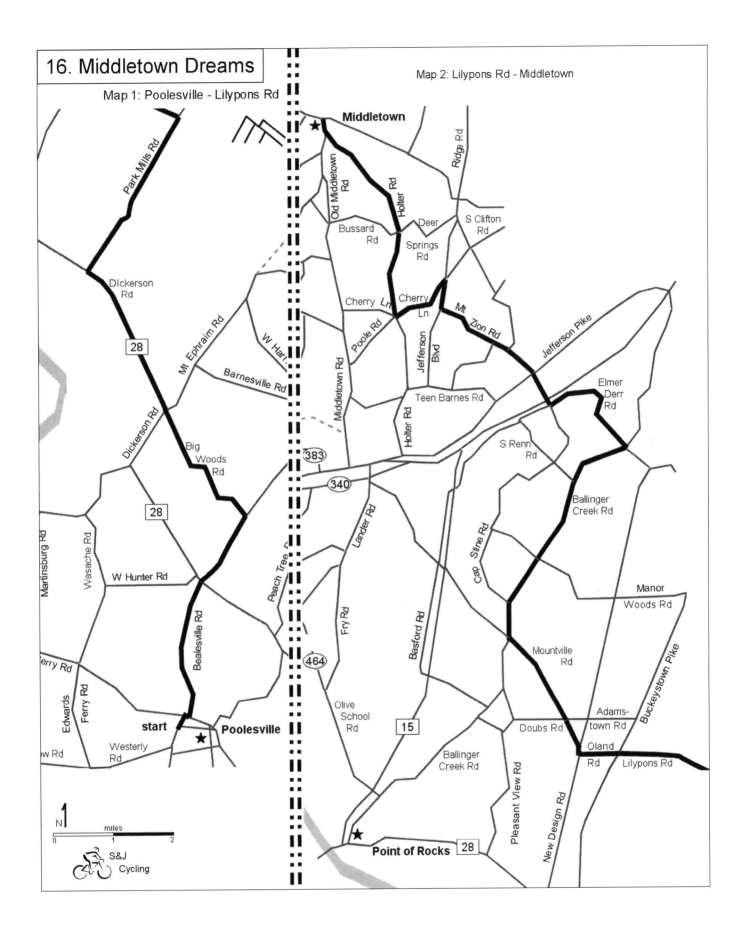

17. Hill Climber's Delight

Distance:	30 or **40** miles
Rating:	IV/V
Start:	Point of Rocks Train Station in Point of Rocks, Md.

40 Mile Ride (V)

0.0	L	28 from parking
0.3	L	15 at T ☹
0.7	R	672, Lovettsville Rd, b/c 673 in **Lovettsville**
7.0	R	287, Berlin Pk ☹; b/c 17, Petersville Rd in **Brunswick**
10.9	S	79, Petersville Rd at SL
12.7	L	180 at T
13.0 ☞*	R	Catholic Church Rd
15.7	L	Gapland Rd
18.1	R	Arnoldstown Rd at top of climb (water)
20.3	L	Picnic Woods Rd at T
22.8	R	Bidle Rd; b/c Walnut St
24.5	BR	Main St at SS in **Middletown** (store)
24.7	R	7, South Church St at SL
25.3	L	Old Middletown Rd
25.7	R	Roy Schafer Rd
26.2	L	Bussard Rd
26.7	R	Old Middletown Rd at T
30.7 ☞*	L	180 at T in **Jefferson**
31.1	R	Lander Rd
31.3	L	Mountville Rd after rte 340 (store)
33.3	R	Basford Rd, just before 15 on downhill
36.5	R	Ballenger Creek Rd at T
40.0	L	28 at T in **Point of Rocks**
40.2	R	to parking

*30 Mile Ride (IV)

15.7	R	Gapland Rd
17.9	S	383, Broad Run Rd a St Marks Rd
20.2	L	180, Jefferson Pike. Rejoin long ride in 0.8 miles at 31.1 turn

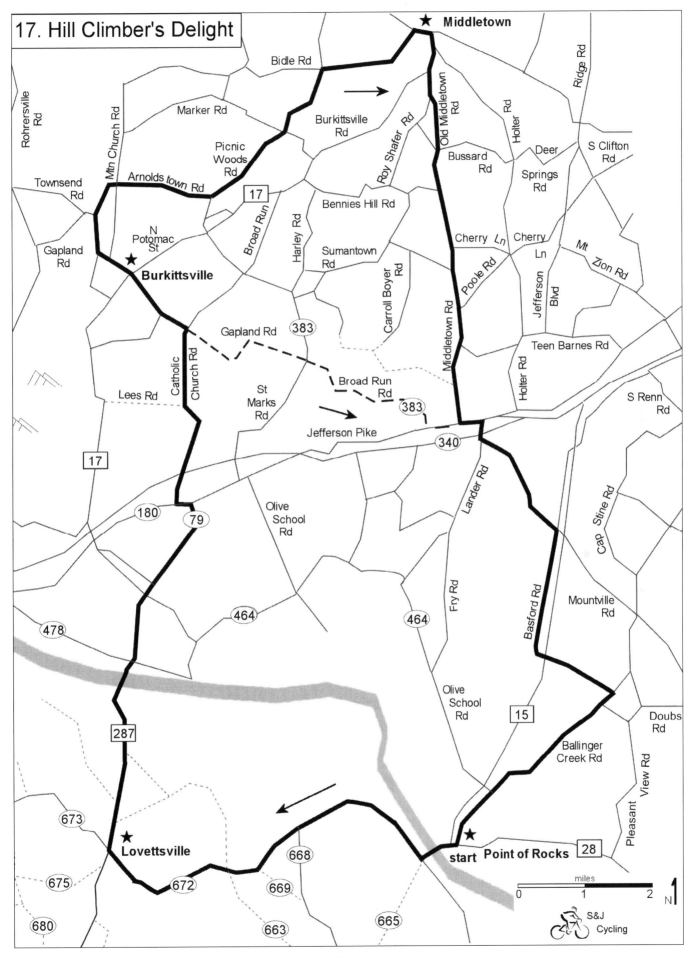

17. Hill Climber's Delight

Middletown

Bidle Rd

Rohrersville Rd

Marker Rd

Mtn Church Rd

Picnic Woods Rd

Burkittsville Rd

Roy Shafer Rd

Old Middletown Rd

Holter Rd

Ridge Rd

Deer

S Clifton Rd

Townsend Rd

Arnolds town Rd

17

Bennies Hill Rd

Bussard Rd

Springs Rd

N Potomac St

Gapland Rd

Burkittsville

Broad Run

Harley Rd

Sumantown Rd

Carroll Boyer Rd

Cherry Ln

Cherry Ln

Mt Zion Rd

Poole Rd

Jefferson Blvd

Catholic Church Rd

Gapland Rd

383

Middletown Rd

Teen Barnes Rd

Lees Rd

St Marks Rd

Broad Run Rd

383

Holter Rd

S Renn Rd

Jefferson Pike

340

17

Olive School Rd

Lander Rd

Cap Stine Rd

180

79

464

464

Fry Rd

Basford Rd

Mountville Rd

478

Olive School Rd

15

Doubs Rd

287

Ballinger Creek Rd

Pleasant View Rd

673

Lovettsville

start   Point of Rocks

28

675

672

668

669

665

680

663

miles
0   1   2

N

S&J Cycling

63

Nokesville region

If there were a "Ride Headquarters" for S&J Cycling, it would probably be located in the Nokesville region. More often than not, if we can't decide on a particular ride, we all agree to meet in Nokesville because it offers a multitude of rides of varying length and difficulty. Many are among our very favorites—WEST OF NOKESVILLE (#21) has been a "standard" for many years, and you will not find a more picturesque ride anywhere than SOUTHERN VIEWS (#33) out of Warrenton.

Legend

20. Smutny's Delight
21. West of Nokesville
22. Nokesville #9
23. Stafford Loop
24. Rural Pleasures
25. Some Hill in Nokesville
26. Shooting the Breeze

31. Short Warrenton
32. East of Warrenton
33. Southern Views
34. Blue Ridge Views
35. King of Swain

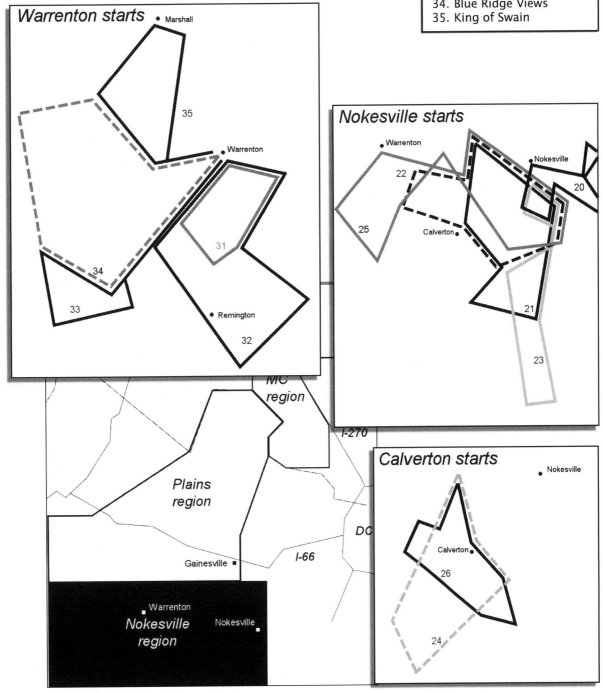

20. Smutny's Delight

Distance *mi*	31.5	39.0
Category	I	I
Climbing *ft*	1379	1815
Rel. climb *ft/mi*	43.8	46.5

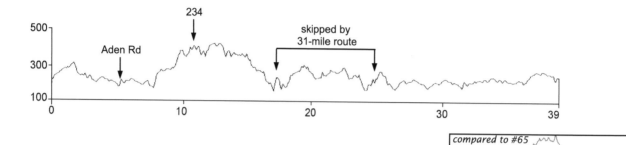

Start Nokesville Community Park in Nokesville, Va.

Route Smutny's Delight is a figure-eight course that opens and closes on very-lightly-trafficked roads, but has a few sections in the middle that have a few too many cars at times. The opening six miles are excellent and lightly traveled by cars. Aden Road has some traffic, which generally increases as the day ages. The first, and thankfully very short, stretch of 234 can be very bad with cars when there is a soccer game at the park. Bristow Road is an improvement, but has little shoulder at first. It's a fun road to ride because it tends downhill. The long route turns off on Lucasville Road toward Manassas, uses another (nasty) stretch of 234, and then parallels back on Brentsville Road. The remainder is 619 is good and has a decent shoulder. After the turn onto 611 at mile 28, the ride returns to the light-traffic zone.

Notes Named for our friend Dave because the ride is so flat (his favorite kind!), the ride is suffering a bit from the encroachment of Manassas-area development. Best done in the early mornings, parts are still gorgeous. Despite the traffic in parts, we like this ride for its use of so many roads found only on this ride.

21. West of Nokesville

Distance *mi*	29.5	43.2
Category	I	I
Climbing *ft*	1319	1955
Rel. climb *ft/mi*	44.7	45.3

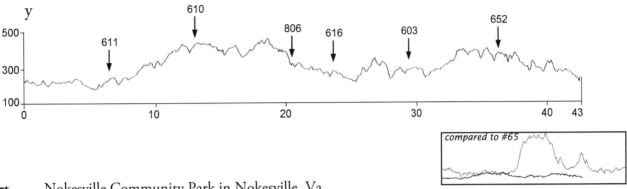

Start   Nokesville Community Park in Nokesville, Va.

Route   Of the rides in this book, the one we've ridden the most is either this one or THE PLAINS (#42). Both provide good roads and distances you can ride year round. NOKESVILLE begins with a three-mile section of Aden Road. If traffic is an issue, try reversing the closing miles of SMUTNY'S DELIGHT (#20)—go right on Carriage Ford Road about ¼-mile from the park in 2.5 miles go left on Hazelwood Drive, then after a bit over 2 miles go right on Fleetwood Drive at the T.

Notes   Nokesville is another classic that has held up well over the years. This was the first S&J ride, with Jim on his DeRosa, Scott on his much missed blue Cannondale, and Dave on his Merckx. The route is flat but for a few rolling hills in the last dozen miles. For us, the addition of several new routes from this start point has revitalized the Nokesville area, and although development is a continuing threat, this route has (so far) survived.

A Chuck & Gail ride.

22. Nokesville #9

Distance *mi*	42.5
Category	I
Climbing *ft*	1942
Rel. climb *ft/mi*	45.7

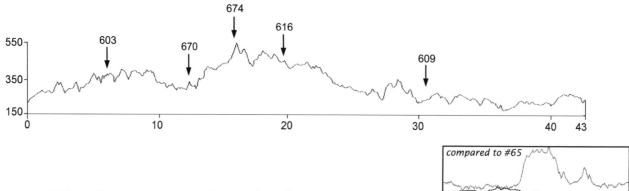

Start   Nokesville Community Park in Nokesville, Va.

Route   Sometimes, alliteration is all—thus the name. Seeking more Nokesville area routes, we came up with this one. It opens by reversing the original WEST OF NOKESVILLE then takes 616 through Casanova—the eastern stretch of which is particularly nice. Southeast of Calverton, it again reverses the original, before returning to the park via the now traditional "back way." The ride is fairly flat with light traffic everywhere but the very beginning.

Notes   What we call the "back way" is a later-developed alternative to a section of a ride. Aden Road southbound has tolerable traffic but northbound later in the day, we prefer to stay off it.

23. Stafford Loop

Distance *mi*		45.9	51.9
Category		II	II
Climbing *ft*		2085	2466
Rel. climb *ft/mi*		45.4	47.5

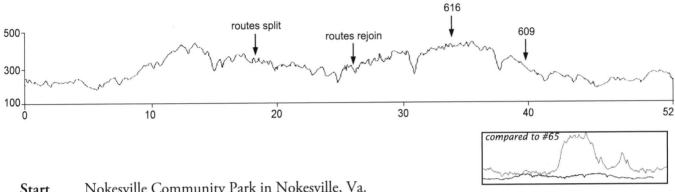

Start Nokesville Community Park in Nokesville, Va.

Route This is a beautiful ride heading south from Nokesville. It tracks the original NOKESVILLE course for the first thirteen miles, then continues south into Stafford County when the original ride turns west. The remarkably nice roads hit their peak with 616, which has smooth pavement and very few cars. The return to Nokesville Community Park is via the Hazelwood Drive-Carriage Ford Road alternative to Aden Roadz. The course is quite flat, like all Nokesville area rides.

Notes The so-called "back way" to and from the start point holds a special place in S&J lore: this stretch of pavement is noted for Jim's infamous "full contact" with a dog back in 2001.

This route has been one of our very favorites since we first rode it. Scott is especially fond of it: he sprung his new frame (the red "antique" Cannondale on the cover) on Team Cholesterol on this course and ruled the day.

24. Rural Pleasures

Distance *mi*	29.7	47.5
Category	I	I
Climbing *ft*	1406	2124
Rel. climb *ft/mi*	47.3	44.7

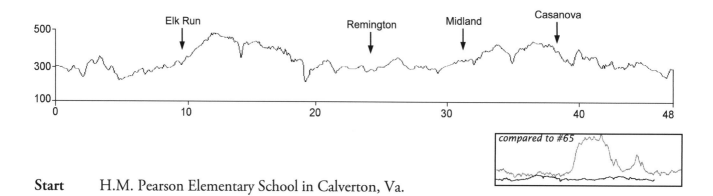

Start   H.M. Pearson Elementary School in Calverton, Va.

Route   The route heads out from the school, surrounded by farms and cow pastures, and heads south in the opening portion of the ride. The hills are few and relatively short, although the steady uphill at Elk Run just past mile ten will give your legs a quick test. From there, the road trends downward until past the halfway point at Remington, where you begin to encounter some small grades on your way to the familiar crossing of the railroad tracks in Casanova. The closing ten miles provide an opportunity for a relatively easy spin as you make your way through scenic farmland back into Calverton.

Notes   This is another excellent ride in the flats around Nokesville. The long version tracks part of the both the long version of EAST OF WARRENTON (on 651), although in reverse, and the short version of that ride (Remington to Midland). This ride is great for a recovery ride or for one of those days where your legs are not quite up to par.

A Chuck & Gail ride.

25. Some Hill in Nokesville

Distance *mi*	63.6
Category	II
Climbing *ft*	3297
Rel. climb *ft/mi*	51.8

Start   Nokesville Community Park in Nokesville, Va.

Route   The Nokesville start point is one of our favorites, but lacks any hills. This ride heads west to Warrenton to provide a few hills and more distance. Instead of using "back way" out of Nokesville, it takes Parkgate Road to the familiar Fleetwood Road. After turning west on 611, it heads northwest for nine miles and the little bridge north of Casanova. The following section around Warrenton provides a few hills. The ride flattens out again after crossing Route 29, before closing with the small rollers on 652.

Notes   This is our longest route from Nokesville—a figure-8 with a few hills thrown in near Warrenton to liven things up a little. This western half of this ride is SHORT WARRENTON (#31). The ride features a fair amount of roads not used in other rides, so it provides some welcome variety out of one of the most convenient start locations.

26. Shooting the Breeze

Distance *mi*	38.8
Category	I
Climbing *ft*	1778
Rel. climb *ft/mi*	45.8

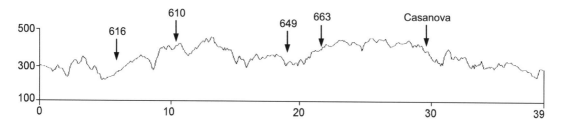

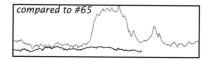

Start   H.M. Pearson Elementary School in Calverton, Va.

Route   This route briefly tracks our other Calverton start (#24, RURAL PLEASURES), before that route bends to the southwest towards Remington. This route continues heading southeast for a few miles before turning northwest and paralleling the opening stretch, heading through Elk Run and Midland. The closing miles on 602 between Casanova and the bridge can be fun, featuring some decent short hills that can liven up the finish if your group is feeling feisty.

Notes   We always seem to do this ride early in the spring or late in the fall. One thing characterizes those two times around here—wind! A day with strong gusts makes this ride much more challenging than the map suggests because you are frequently riding into the wind on exposed roads for long stretches of time. Tail winds can be an excuse to lollygag (as our friend Michael accused us of one fine day, thinking we were shooting the breeze rather than pushing it), but you build strength quicker if you ride smartly no matter what the wind is doing. After all, a headwind likely awaits you around the next corner and getting motivated to work hard into the wind after you've been sailing with the wind can be difficult.

31. Short Warrenton

Distance *mi*	32.4
Category	II
Climbing *ft*	1815
Rel. climb *ft/mi*	56.0

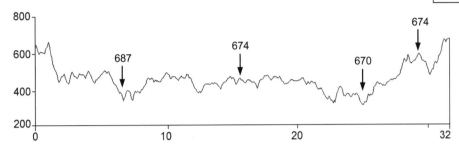

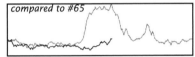

Start   Municipal parking lot in Warrenton, Va.

Route   This ride is the western loop of SOME HILL IN NOKESVILLE (#25). The ride begins easy, with the first six-and-a-half miles generally downhill. The middle section is generally flat, and then in the closing seven miles you regain the elevation that made the opening part of the ride so much fun.

Notes   While not a ride we choose frequently, it can provide a nice taste of the Warrenton area for cyclists who enjoy getting out of the city but don't want to put in forty or fifty miles in doing so. And while this ride is relatively short, it does provide a few decent hills just to make sure your legs feel the effort! A good ride for a lazy Sunday—little traffic, beautiful roads, and a nice climb in the last six miles that will give you a chance to show your stuff and finish strong!

32. East of Warrenton

Distance _mi_	42.7	53.0	57.9
Category	II	II	II
Climbing _ft_	2213	2719	3037
Rel. climb _ft/mi_	51.8	52.3	52.5

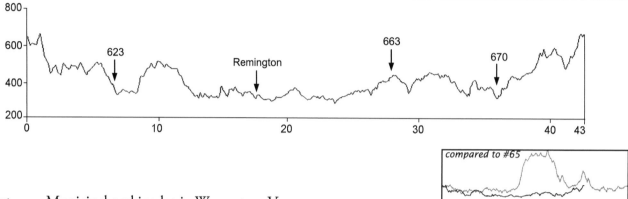

Start   Municipal parking lot in Warrenton, Va.

Route   The ride opens easy with the downhill trend of 802. Heading into Remington on 621 and 651 is fun, with a few small rollers to liven things up. The short route takes 656 while the longer routes loop south and rejoin in Midland. The short and the long route then pass by Casanova. All three meet again on 670 and do the last small climb back to Warrenton.

Notes   We developed this ride back in 1999 and have used it consistently ever since. The Warrenton start provides some nice variety and the three distance options cover all stages of the cycling season. The ride always seems fresh thanks to the beautiful roads and scenery that are featured throughout. Several flat sections in the middle of the ride provide a great opportunity for a steady paceline if you're riding with a good group where all want to share the work. Catch a day with the wind at your back and see how easy it is for a paceline to maintain speeds well over 20 mph! Don't worry, the last seven miles are easier than they look—at least in Scott's opinion!

33. Southern Views

Distance *mi*	53.8
Category	IV
Climbing *ft*	3989
Rel. climb *ft/mi*	74.1

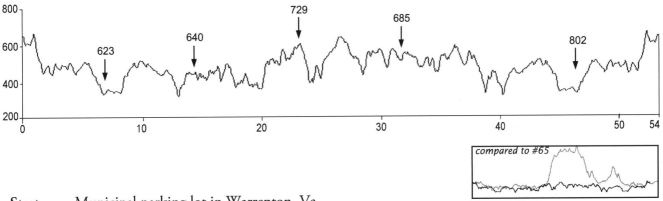

Start   Municipal parking lot in Warrenton, Va.

Route   This is a lovely ride into rarely traveled territory north of Culpeper. Traffic is generally light, except on 729. The ride does not appear to rate a IV rating in the first half, but the last ten miles are much harder, traversing the upward-trending rollers (a.k.a. the "gentle downhills" in jest) back into Warrenton.

Notes   We really love this ride for its scenic beauty and the consistently high quality of the roads you encounter as you make your way south from Warrenton and then enjoy a loop through very small towns with picturesque names like Rixeyville. Perhaps its just luck, but neither Scott nor Jim can remember a "bad" day on this route—indeed, the sun typically shines and winds are light. Try it and see if this good fortune falls on you as well—no matter what, we guarantee you're bound to agree this is an especially sweet ride!

34. Blue Ridge Views

Distance *mi*	60.2
Category	V
Climbing *ft*	4746
Rel. climb *ft/mi*	78.8

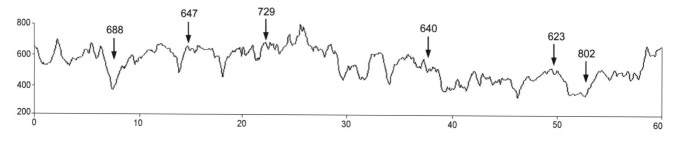

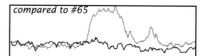

Start   Municipal parking lot in Warrenton, Va.

Route   The route quickly leaves Warrenton behind and by mile seven, as you turn on to Route 688, the
scenery becomes decidedly rural. A store is strategically located in Flint Hill just shy of the halfway
point and provides an opportunity to stock up on fluids or your energy bar of choice.

Notes   This was the first of our Warrenton rides and one that still gives us pause. The only category V ride
without a signature climb, the constant rollers that mark this course will wear you down nonetheless.
Atypically, the route departs Warrenton on Waterloo Street. Light traffic prevails through most of the
ride.

The route returns to Warrenton via the infamous "gentle downhills" of 802. Somehow we got the
idea that Chuck & Gail's description of the closing stretch on 802 called it "gentle downhills." We
laughed at this complete mischaracterization for years, until we checked their description and found
no such phrase. By tradition on our team, Jim has to tow everyone up the last climb into town. While
Scott generally likes hills, Jim's second-half strength usually tips the scales in his favor.

A Chuck & Gail ride.

35. King of Swain

Distance *mi*	41.3
Category	IV
Climbing *ft*	3253
Rel. climb *ft/mi*	79.0

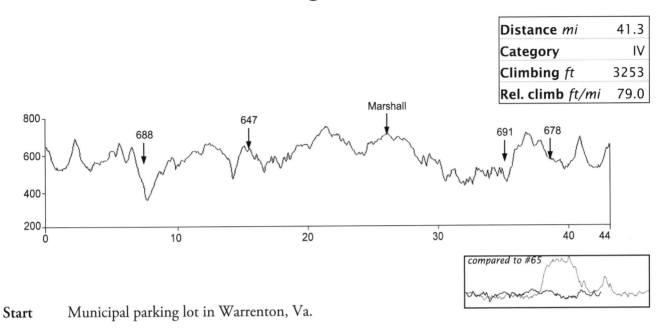

Start Municipal parking lot in Warrenton, Va.

Route Named for Swains' Mountain, an East-coast "mountain" bracketed by 691 and 647 and circled by this ride, this ride looks rather Hobbsian. Almost the only flat roads on this ride are in Marshall, but the hills seems easier than others, such as westbound on 635 (used in BUG, SWEAT & TEARS and STORMIN' THE GAP). The crossing of 211 on the return is blocked by a median—our best solution is to walk the bikes across the street. Overall, this is a hilly but rewarding ride.

Notes This is a great ride for practically any part of the cycling season. Lots of hills to get your heart rate up, particularly if someone in your group (in our group it always seems to be Scott or Michael) is feeling feisty and forcing the others to do battle to the top of every climb! Thankfully, it ends rather quickly, so you can thrash each other on the hills and still make it back to the car without hitting empty. In the early part of the year it provides a nice ride for that stage in your season where you're ready for some steady hills but can't quite face up to the Marshall routes.

20. Smutny's Delight

Distance:	31 or **39** miles
Rating:	I
Start:	Nokesville Community Park in Nokesville, Va.

39 Mile Ride

0.1	L	646, Aden Rd
1.5	R	671, Colvin Lane
3.4	R	611, Valley View Dr at T
4.4	R	653, Parkgate Dr at T
4.6	L	611, Fleetwood Dr
6.3	L	646, Aden Rd at SS
12.4	L	619, Joplin Rd
12.6	L	234, Dumfries Rd ☹
13.0	BL	619, Bristow Rd (park with bathrooms on left)
☞ *		
17.6	R	692, Lucasville Rd
17.7	BL	692, Lucasville Rd
20.9	R	Hastings Dr at T
21.3	R	234, Dumfries Rd ☹

22.6	BR	TRO 234
22.8	R	649, Brentsville Rd
25.1	L	692, Lucasville Rd at T
25.2 ☞ *	R	619, Bristow Rd
28.2	L	611, Valley View Dr
30.8	R	653, Parkgate Rd at T
31.1	L	611, Fleetwood Dr (cross Aden Rd at 32.7 mi)
34.2	R	645, Hazelwood Dr
36.4	R	607, Carriage Ford Rd at T
38.8	L	646, Aden Rd at T
39.0	L	Nokesville Community Park

*31 Mile Ride

20.7	L	611, Valley View Dr
23.3	R	653, Parkgate Rd at T
23.7	L	611, Fleetwood Dr (cross Aden Rd at mi 25.2)
26.7	R	645, Hazelwood Dr

28.9	R	607, Carriage Ford Rd at T
31.3	L	646, Aden Rd at T
31.5	L	Nokesville Community Park

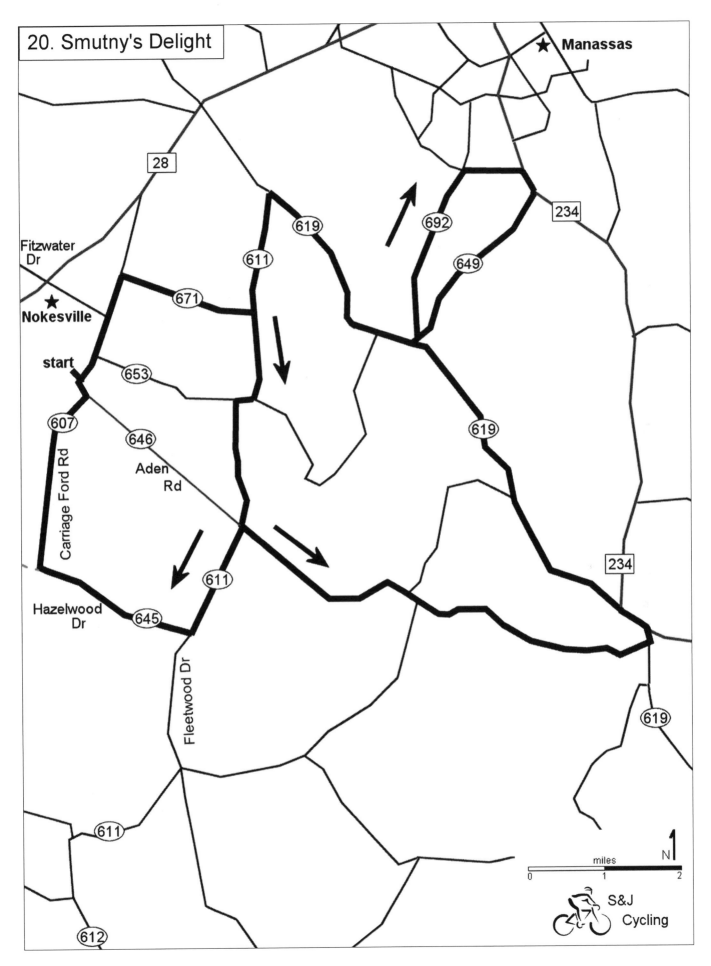

20. Smutny's Delight

Manassas

28

Fitzwater Dr

Nokesville

start

619

611

692

234

649

671

653

607

Carriage Ford Rd

646

Aden Rd

619

234

611

Hazelwood Dr

645

Fleetwood Dr

619

611

612

miles
0 1 2

N

S&J Cycling

21. (West of) Nokesville

Distance:	30 or **43** miles
Rating:	I
Start:	Nokesville Community Park in Nokesville, Va.

43 Mile Ride

0.1	R	646, Aden Rd		30.0	S	603 at SS in **Calverton** (store)
3.1	R	611, Fleetwood Dr		33.1	R	667 at T
6.4	R	611 at T		33.3	L	603 at T (store at mi 35.7)
8.2 ☞*	BL	612		36.8	R	652
13.6	R	610/612 & immediately		38.1	R	604, Burwell Rd at T
13.6	BR	610		38.2	L	652, Fitzwater Dr
16.4	L	616 at T		42.4	R	646, Aden Rd at T
16.6	R	610 in **Somerville** (store)		43.2	R	to parking
21.0	R	806 in **Elk Run** (store)				
25.0 ☞*	L	616				

*30 Mile Ride

9.0	R	609 from 612		11.4	R	616. Rejoin long route in 5.0 miles at 30.0 turn
10.8	L	806 at SS in **Bristerburg**				

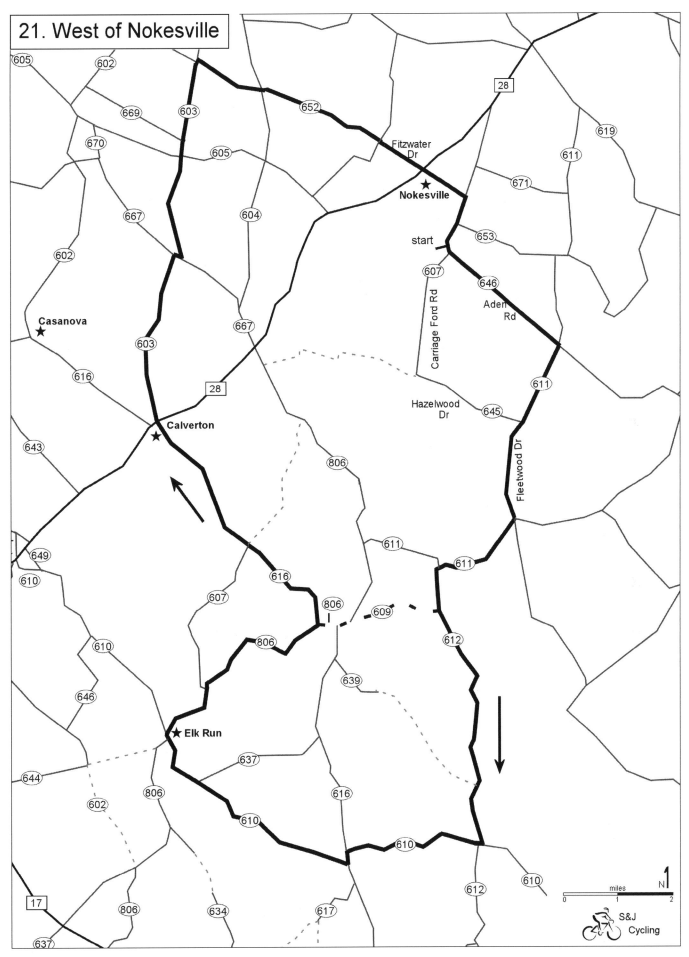

21. West of Nokesville

81

22. Nokesville #9

Distance:	43 miles
Rating:	II
Start:	Nokesville Community Park in Nokesville, Va.

0.2	L	646, Aden Rd from parking
1.0	L	652, Fitzwater Dr
5.3	R	604, Burwell Rd at T
5.4	L	652
6.7	L	603 at SS (store at mi 8.3)
10.2	R	667
12.6	L	670
13.1	BL	602/670 to cross bridge
13.2	R	670 at T
16.3	L	674. Unpaved for 0.2 miles
17.1	X	643
19.6	BL	TRO 674, Green Rd
19.8	L	616
21.6	R	643 at T
21.8	L	616
25.6	L	28 ☹
25.7	R	616 in **Calverton** (store)
30.8	L	806 at T
31.4	BR	609 in **Bristerburg**
33.2	L	612 at T
34.0	BR	611
35.8	L	611, Fleetwood Dr
37.7	L	645, Hazelwood Dr
39.8	R	607, Carriage Ford Rd at T
42.3	L	646, Aden Rd at T
42.5	L	Nokesville Community Park

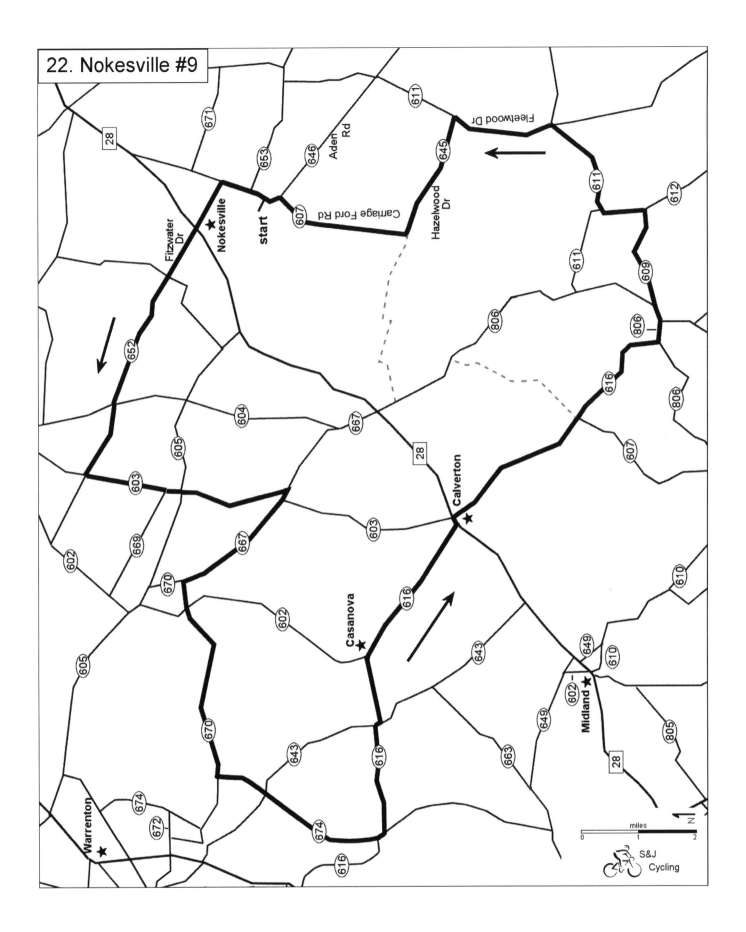

23. Stafford Loop

Distance:	**46** or 52 miles
Rating:	II
Start:	Nokesville Community Park in Nokesville, Va.

46 Mile Ride

0.1	R	646, Aden Rd		26.5	R	614 at 615
3.1	R	611, Fleetwood Dr		28.3	L	616 at T
6.4	R	611 at T		34.6	R	806 at SS
8.2	BL	612		34.9	BR	609
13.6	R	610/612 & immediately		36.6	L	612 at T
13.6	BL	612		37.5	BR	611
15.5	S	646, Tacketts Mill Rd		39.3	L	611
17.0	L	616 at T		41.1	L	645, Hazelwood Dr
☞*						
17.8	BR	616 at 627 (store)		43.3	R	607, Carriage Ford Rd at T
☞*						
20.5	R	662		45.7	L	646, Aden Rd at T
23.3	R	612 at T		45.9	L	Nokesville Community Park
24.3	BL	614 at Y at 612				

*52 Mile Ride

17.8	L	627, Mountain View Rd		26.1	R	616, Poplar Rd at T
22.5	R	648, Stefaniga Rd		26.5	L	662

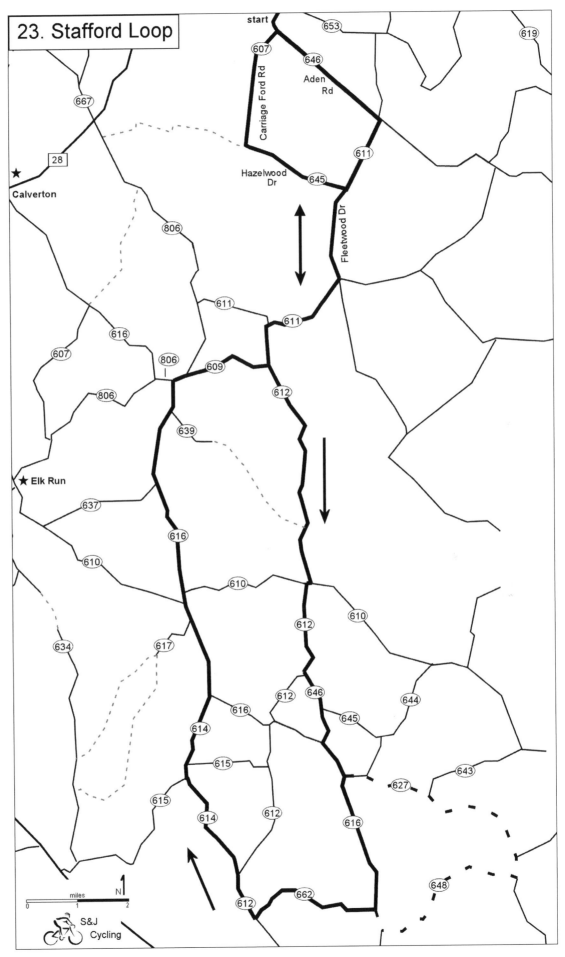

23. Stafford Loop

start

607
653
619
646

Carriage Ford Rd

Aden Rd

611

Hazelwood Dr
645

Fleetwood Dr

667

28

Calverton

806

611

611

616

607

806

612

639

Elk Run

637

616

610

610

612

610

634

617

616

612

646

614

645

644

616

615

627
643

615

614

612

616

614

662

612

648

miles
0   1   2

N

S&J
Cycling

24. Rural Pleasures

Distance:	30 or **47** miles
Rating:	I
Start:	H.M. Pearson Elementary School in Calverton, Va.

47 Mile Ride

0.0	L	603 from parking lot		31.3	L	602
0.9	S	616 at 28 in **Calverton**		31.9	L	649 at SS ☞*
5.9	R	806 at T ☜*		33.7	R	663, Balls Mill Rd at T
12.8	R	637		35.8	L	643 at T
15.6	R	637 at 634		37.0	R	616, Casanova Rd
17.6	R	651 at SS		38.2	L	747 to cross RR tracks in **Casanova**
24.3	R	656, Franklin St in **Remington**		38.2	L	602, Rogues Rd
24.6	R	656		41.7	R	602/670 to cross bridge
27.8	R	661 at SS		41.8	BR	670
27.8	L	805		42.3	R	667 at Y
30.4	L	602 at T		44.5	R	603
31.0	L	610 at T		46.8	L	to parking lot
31.2	R	28 in **Midland**				

*30 Mile Ride

9.9	R	610 in **Elk Run**		13.8	S	649

rejoin 47-mi ride in 2.8 miles at 33.7 mile turn

24. Rural Pleasures

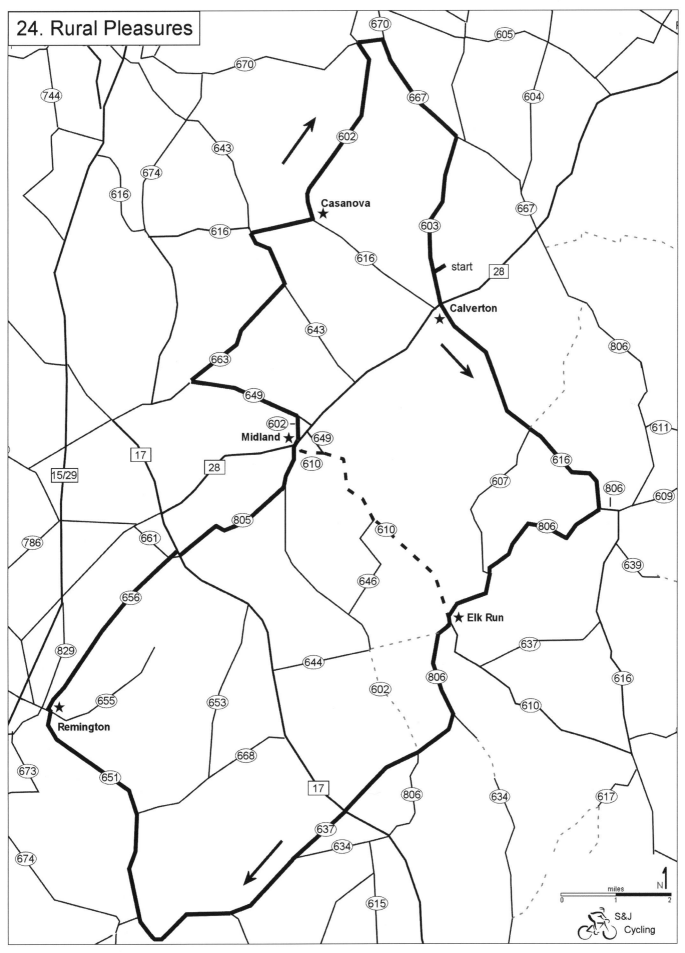

25. Some Hill in Nokesville

Distance:	64 miles
Rating:	II
Start:	Nokesville Community Park in Nokesville, Va.

0.2	L	646, Aden Rd
0.6	R	653, Parkgate Rd
2.6	R	611, Fleetwood Dr
4.2	X	646, Aden Rd at SS (store)
7.5	R	611 at T (unmarked)
9.2	R	611, Swego Rd (612 goes straight)
10.8	R	806, Elk Run Rd at T
15.2	X	28 at SL. B/c 667, Old Dumfries Rd
17.4	L	TRO 667, Old Dumfries Rd at 603
19.7	L	670, Old Auburn Rd at SS
20.2	L	TRO 670 and cross bridge
20.3	R	670 at T
24.5	R	674, Frytown Rd
25.2	L	672, Dunhollow Rd
25.6	R	643, Meetze Rd at SS ☹
26.4	S	E Lee St at SS in **Warrenton**
26.8	L	Culpeper St. B/c 802, Springs Rd at SL
33.4	L	687, Opal Rd
35.7	R	685, Routts Hill Rd
37.3	R	651, Lees Mill Rd
38.3	BL	661, Botha Rd
39.9	L	663, Covingtons Corner Rd
40.7	X	29
41.7	X	17
41.8	BR	663
41.9	L	TRO 663, Balls Mill Rd
42.5	L	674, Green Rd
45.6	R	616, Beach Rd
47.5	R	643, Meetze Rd
47.6	L	616, Casanova Rd
48.8	L	747, Weston Rd (RR tracks) in **Casanova**
48.9	L	602, Rogues Rd
52.3	R	670 over bridge
52.4	L	602 (first left after bridge)
53.4	R	605, Dumfries Rd at T
55.3	L	603, Greenwich Rd
57.0	R	652, Kennedy Rd
58.3	R	604, Burwell Rd at T
58.4	L	652, Fitzwater Dr
61.7	X	28 at SL
62.6	R	646, Aden Rd at T
63.4	R	to parking

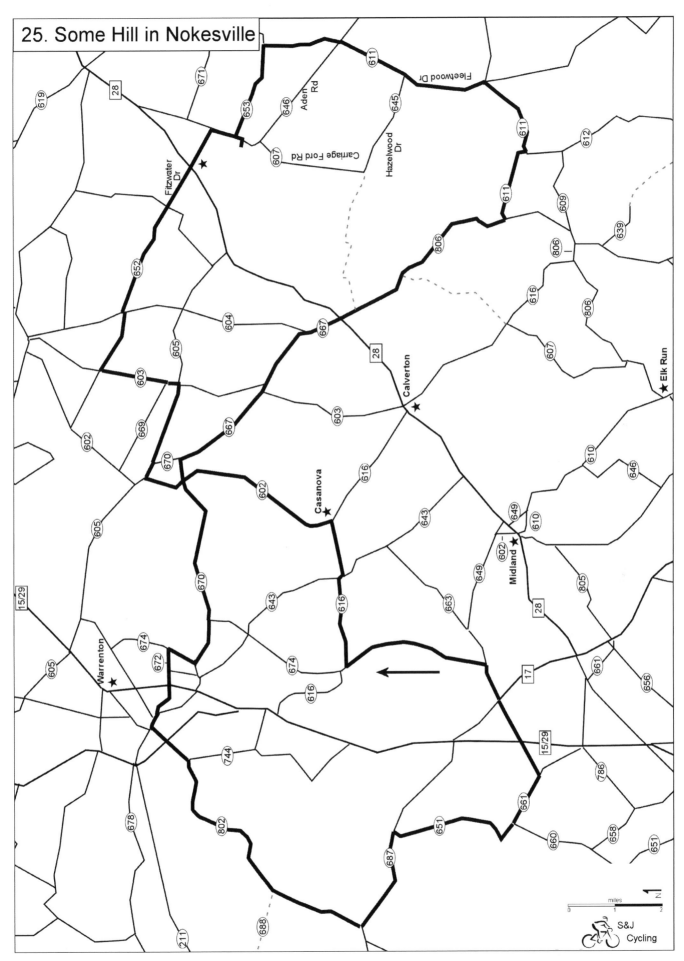

26. Shooting the Breeze

Distance:	39 miles
Rating:	I
Start:	H.M. Pearson Elementary School in Calverton, Va.

0.0	L	603 from parking lot
0.9	S	616 at 28 in **Calverton**
5.9	L	806 at T
6.3	R	616
11.0	R	610
15.6	X	806 in **Elk Run** (store)
19.5	S	649
22.3	L	663, Balls Mill Rd at T
23.7	R	674
26.9	R	616

28.8	R	643 at T
29.0	L	616
30.2	L	747 to cross RR tracks in **Casanova**
30.2	L	602, Rogues Rd
33.7	R	602/670 to cross bridge
33.8	BR	670
34.3	R	667 at Y
36.5	R	603
38.8	L	to parking lot

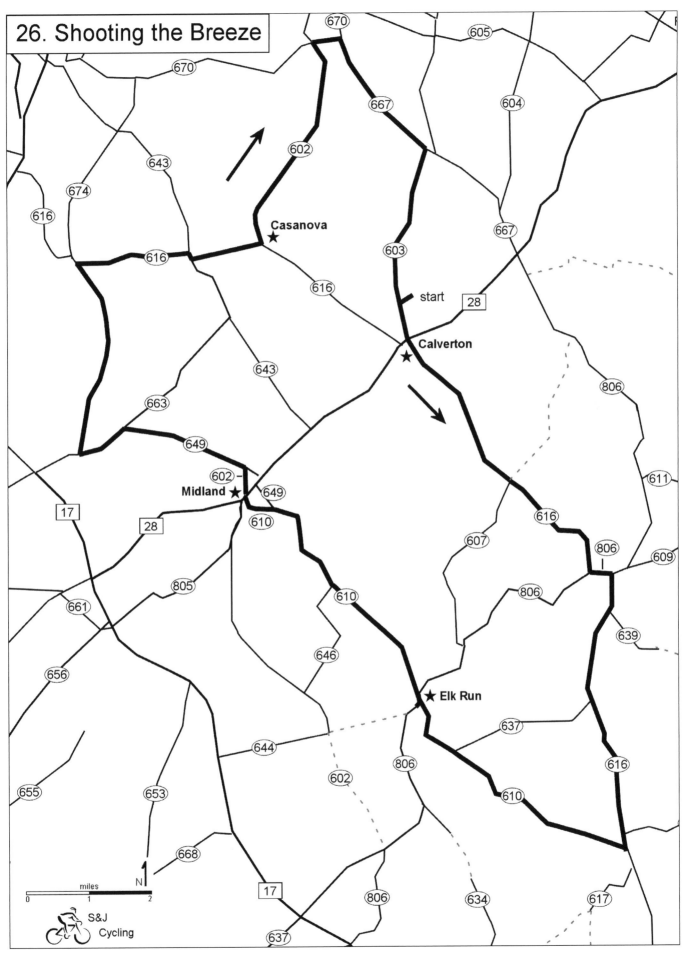

26. Shooting the Breeze

Casanova

Calverton

start

Midland

Elk Run

miles
0 1 2

N

S&J
Cycling

31. Short Warrenton

Distance:	32 miles
Rating:	II
Start:	Municipal Parking Lot in Warrenton, Va.

0.0	L	Franklin St, from back of parking lot	15.9	L	674, Green Rd
0.1	R	Culpeper St. Becomes 802	19.0	R	616, Beach Rd
			20.8	R	643, Meetze Rd
6.6	L	687, Opal Rd	21.0	L	616, Casanova Rd
8.9	R	685, Routts Hill Rd	22.2	L	747, Weston Rd (RR tracks) in **Casanova**
10.5	R	651, Lees Mill Rd			
11.5	BL	661, Botha Rd	22.3	L	602, Rogues Rd
13.1	L	663, Covingtons Corner Rd	25.7	BL	670, bridge on right
			29.8	R	674, Frytown Rd
13.9	X	29	30.4	L	672, Dunhollow Rd
14.9	X	17	30.9	R	643, Meetze Rd
15.0	BR	663	31.8	S	Lee St at SS
15.1	L	TRO 663, Balls Mill Rd	32.4	L	into parking at Ashby St

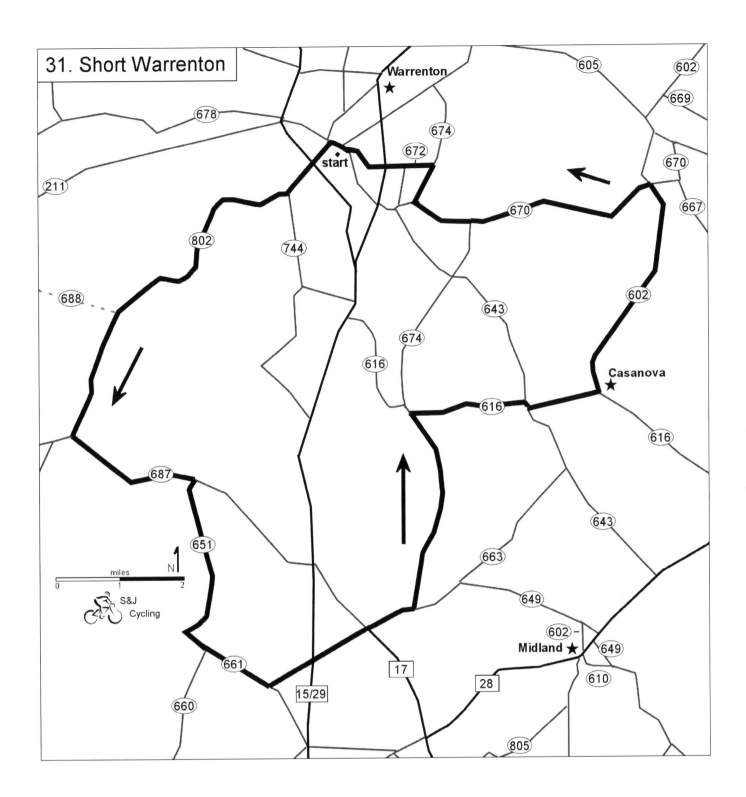

31. Short Warrenton

Warrenton

start

Casanova

Midland

S&J Cycling

miles
0   1   2
N

211
678
674
672
674
670
670
605
602
669
667
670
802
744
688
643
602
616
674
616
616
616
687
651
643
663
649
602
649
610
805
661
660
15/29
17
28

93

32. East of Warrenton

Distance:	43, 52 or **58** miles
Rating:	II
Start:	Municipal Parking Lot in Warrenton, Va.

58 Mile Ride

0.0	L	Franklin St, from parking
0.1	R	Culpeper St from parking. Becomes 802
7.0	L	623, Myers Mill Rd.
9.9	L	621
10.8	L	621 at 625
13.3	S	651
17.8	X	15/29
18.3	X	James Madison Highway in **Remington**.
		☞ * *43-mi route*
18.5	S	Cross RR tracks
25.3	L	637
27.4	L	Shipps Store Rd
28.5	X	17
30.4	L	806 at T
30.5	BR	806, Elk Run Rd
33.2	L	610, Midland Rd in **Elk Run** (store)
37.2	S	649
37.7	X	Rt 28
39.9	L	663, Balls Mill Rd at T
41.2	R	674
		☞ ***52-mi route*
44.4	R	616
46.2	R	643 ☹
46.4	L	616
47.6	L	602 in **Casanova**
		☞ * *43-mi route*
51.2	BL	670, bridge on right
55.3	R	674, Frytown Rd
		☞ ***52-mi route*
55.9	L	672, Dunhollow Rd
56.5	R	643
57.3	S	Lee St at SS
57.9	L	into parking at Ashby St

*43 Mile Ride

18.4	L	656, Franklin St b4 RR tracks
18.8	R	656
22.0	R	661 to cross RR tracks, then
22.0	L	805
24.6	L	602 at T
25.2	L	610 at T
25.4	R	28 in **Midland**
25.5	L	602
26.1	L	649 at SS
27.9	R	663, Balls Mill Rd at T
30.0	L	643 at T
31.2	R	616, Casanova Rd
32.4	L	602, cross over RR tracks, then L on 602, Rogues Rd
		rejoin 58-miler after 47.6

**52 Mile Ride

44.2	S	674 passing 616
44.3	R	674, Lunstold Rd, at 616
46.9	X	643 (L & quick R). Unpaved
47.7	L	670 at T
48.7	R	674, Frytown Rd
		rejoin 58-miler after 55.3 turn

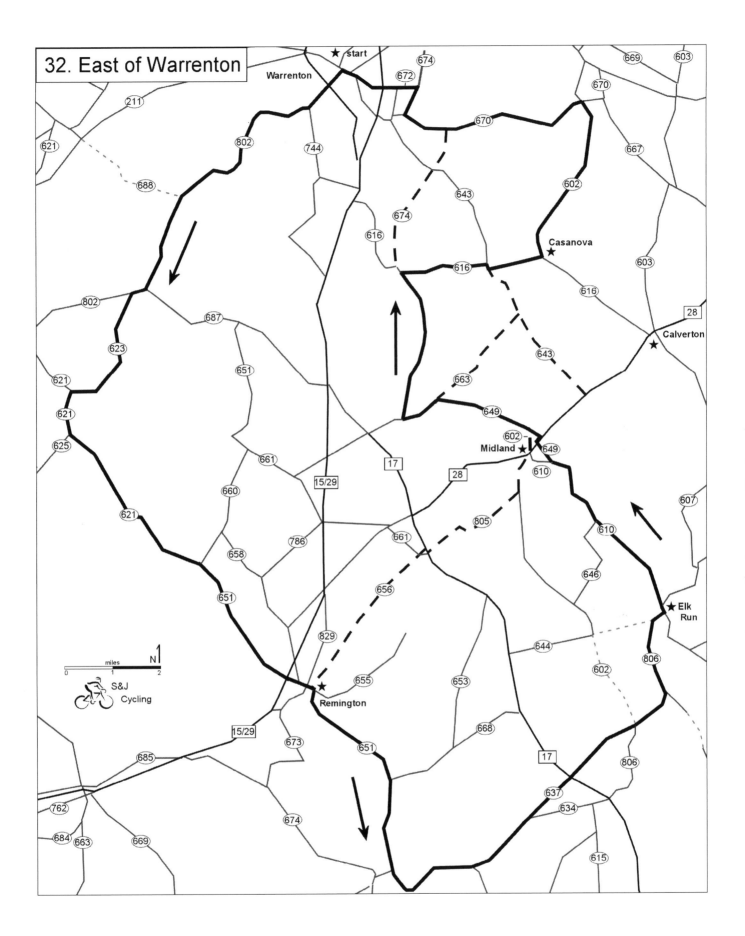

32. East of Warrenton

33. Southern Views

Distance:	54 miles
Rating:	IV
Start:	Municipal Parking Lot in Warrenton, Va.

0.0	L	Franklin St, from back of parking	31.9	BL	685, Crescent Fork Rd
			33.1	S	685 at SS, crossing 229
0.1	R	Culpeper St. Becomes 802	34.4	L	625 at T
7.0	L	623, Myers Mill Rd	39.7	R	625 at T at 640
9.9	L	621	42.9	BL	621
10.8	R	625 at 621	43.9	R	623 at T
14.0	S	640 at 625	46.8	R	802 at T. Becomes Culpeper St in **Warrenton**
17.1	R	229, Rixeyville Rd at T			
17.4	L	640 in **Rixeyville**	53.7	L	Franklin St
21.5	BL	627	53.8	R	to parking
23.4	L	729 at T (store at mi 28.2)			

33. Southern Views

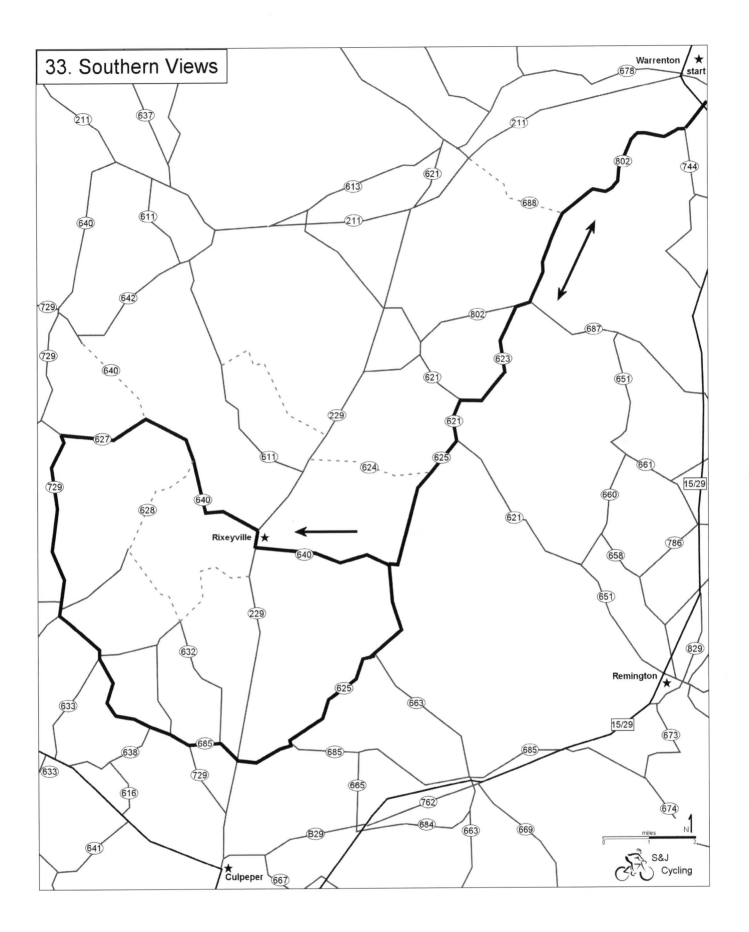

Warrenton ★ start

Culpeper ★

Rixeyville ★

Remington ★

S&J Cycling

97

34. Blue Ridge Views

Distance:	60 miles
Rating:	V
Start:	Municipal parking lot in Warrenton, Va.

0.0	S	Ashby St from parking	35.7	BL	729 at 615
0.1	L	Waterloo St at SS	36.3	L	627 toward Rixeyville
0.8	S	211 at light	38.3	S	640
0.9	R	Rappahannock St	42.4	R	229 at T in **Rixeyville**
0.9	L	Waterloo Rd at SS, becomes 678	42.7	L	640
			45.8	S	625
4.9	L	691	49.1	S	621
7.1	R	688 at SS (store at mi 12.6 in **Orlean**)	50.1	R	623 at T
15.3	L	647	53.0	R	802 at T. Becomes Culpeper St in **Warrenton**
23.1	L	522 at T in **Flint Hill**			
23.5	L	729 toward Ben Venue	60.1	L	Franklin St
32.2	L	729 at SS (store at mi 35.2)	60.2	R	to parking

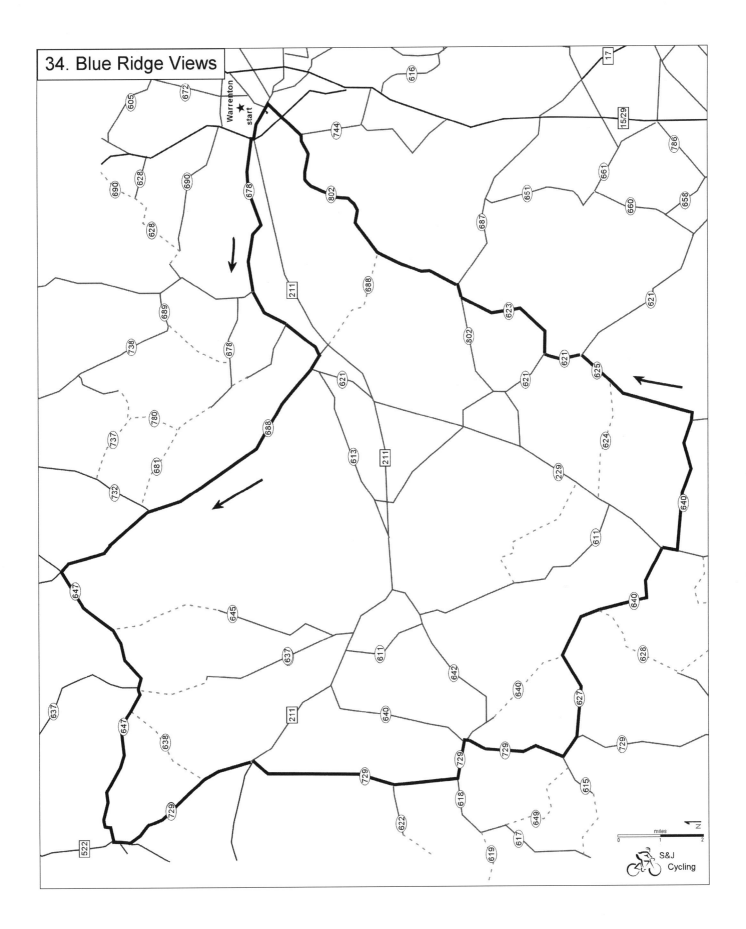

35. King of Swain

Distance:	41 miles
Rating:	IV
Start:	Municipal parking lot in Warrenton, Va.

0.0	S	Ashby St from parking	25.3	R	710/Bus-17 at SL in **Marshall**
0.1	L	Waterloo St at SS			
0.8	S	211 at SL	26.4	R	691, Carter's Run after crossing I-66
0.9	R	Rappahannock St	34.8	L	691, Wilson Rd
0.9	L	Waterloo Rd at SS, becomes 678	37.3	BL	678, Old Waterloo Rd
4.9	L	691	40.4	R	Rappahannock St
7.1	R	688 at SS (store at mi 12.6 in **Orlean**)	40.4	L	211 (walk bikes across median)
15.0	R	647	40.5	R	Waterloo St at SL
24.3	L	647/17 at T	41.2	R	Ashby St
24.6	R	55, Main St	41.3	S	to parking

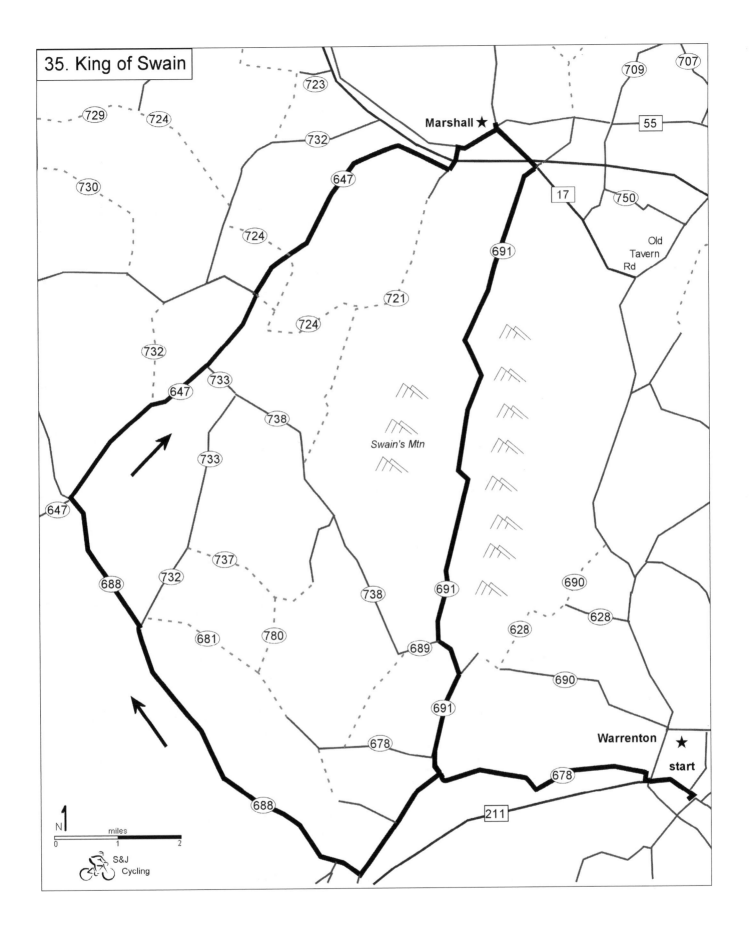

35. King of Swain

729
724
723
709
707
Marshall ★
55
732
647
17
750
730
691
Old Tavern Rd
724
724
721
732
647 733
738
Swain's Mtn
733
737
732
688
738
691
690
628
628
780
681
689
690
691
678
Warrenton ★ start
678
688
211

N
miles
0   1   2
S&J Cycling

The Plains region

Straddled by the Blue Ridge Mountains on the west and the smaller Bull Run Mountain and co. to the east, this region has long been our favorite. The region north of Marshall is relatively flat and yields two "easier" rides: THE MARSHALL PLAN (#62) and BACKWARDS PLAINS (#46). The land south of Marshall is packed with rollers. The Plains region also has both of our "if I could only keep one" rides: THE PLAINS (#42) for Scott and BUG, SWEAT & TEARS (#61) for Jim. None of the Marshall rides head east because we both live near Washington, D.C. If a ride went much east of Marshall, it would run through The Plains and we would start the ride from there.

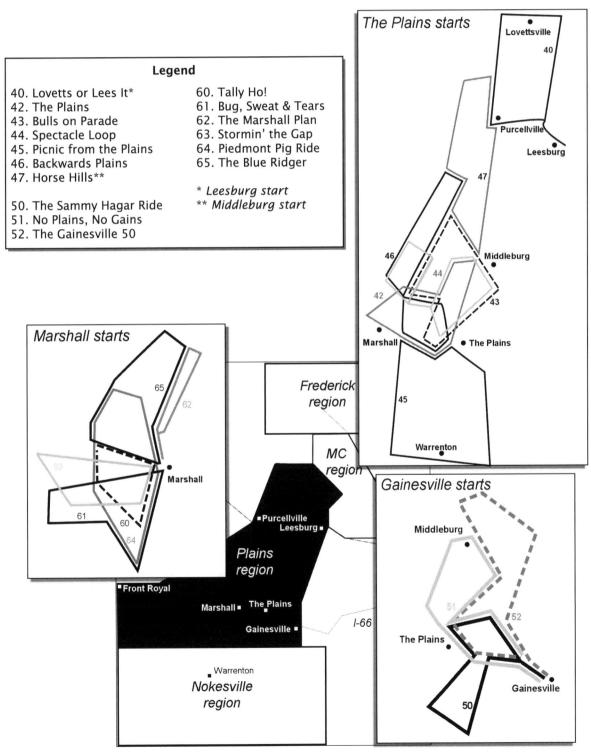

Legend

40. Lovetts or Lees It*
42. The Plains
43. Bulls on Parade
44. Spectacle Loop
45. Picnic from the Plains
46. Backwards Plains
47. Horse Hills**

50. The Sammy Hagar Ride
51. No Plains, No Gains
52. The Gainesville 50

60. Tally Ho!
61. Bug, Sweat & Tears
62. The Marshall Plan
63. Stormin' the Gap
64. Piedmont Pig Ride
65. The Blue Ridger

Leesburg start
** *Middleburg start*

40. Lovetts or Lees It

Distance *mi*		43.1
Category		III
Climbing *ft*		2830
Rel. climb *ft/mi*		65.7

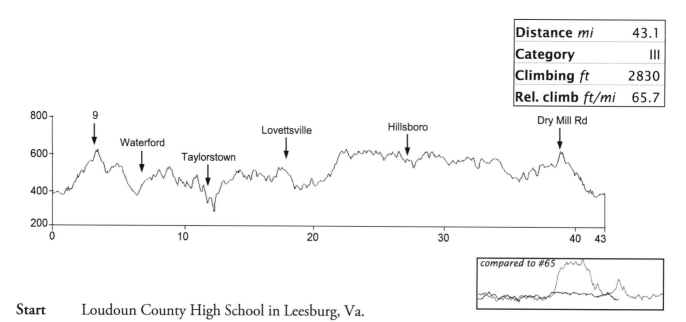

Start   Loudoun County High School in Leesburg, Va.

Route   Although the ride opens with the uphill run on Dry Mill Road, it finishes by reversing the same stretch for a fast finish. After Dry Mill Road, 662 to Waterford has some nice downhill stretches. Route 665 to Taylorstown is a gorgeous road. After Lovettsville, Mountain Road sounds ominous, but the trouble never actually materializes.

Notes   The two halves of this have distinct personalities—the first half is a rollerfest that will have you doubting our rating system, while the second half promises trouble around every corner but never delivers it. The finish down Dry Mill Run is a blast and makes all the early climbing worthwhile.

42. The Plains

Distance *mi*	33.7	39.0
Category	III	III
Climbing *ft*	2212	2664
Rel. climb *ft/mi*	65.6	68.3

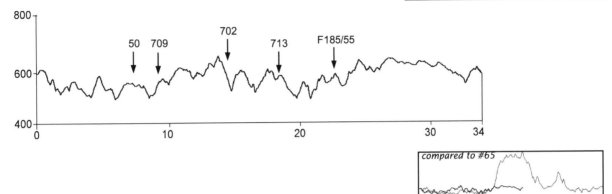

Start   Street parking in The Plains, Va.

Route   The ride begins on 626 toward Middleburg. It then climbs Middleburg hill—the scene of many frenzied uphill sprint battles in our group—runs along Zulla Road and turns west on Frogtown Road—one of Jim's first and still favorite attack points. In Rectortown, the route turns south again toward 55 and a few hills, including "Boo Hill." The stretch from 55 back to The Plains is a flat run on nice pavement. The route seems to have shrunk over the years, but the 39-mile version, which includes a short stretch on 17, has expanded the seasons for this ride.

Notes   Ten years after we first rode this course, it is still one of our very favorites. Not the prettiest or the least-trafficked of our rides, all of its roads have good memories. The opening eight miles on 626 are Scott's favorite stretch of road—the small rollers and curving hills have always been to his liking. Back when he was younger and the quick starter of our group, he used to drop Jim mercilessly on this stretch. Now Michael has assumed that mantle and Scott's voice joins Jim's in complaining about the lack of a warm-up!

Mostly a Chuck & Gail ride.

43. Bulls on Parade

Distance *mi*	34.9	37.7
Category	IV	IV
Climbing *ft*	2701	2785
Rel. climb *ft/mi*	77.4	73.9

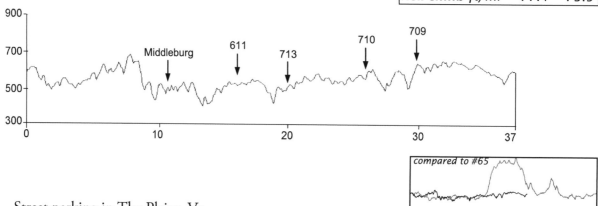

Start   Street parking in The Plains, Va.

Route   Starting from The Plains, this route takes the hillier "back way" into Middleburg (628/686/776). In Middleburg, it continues north on 626 then heads back down to 55 on St. Louis Road—a great road in either direction. After a brief stretch on 50, it continues south on Atoka Road. Frogtown Road leads to 709/Zulla Road. The short route angles toward The Plains on 707 and 704, while the longer route takes Zulla Road down past 50 to 750 and heads back north to The Plains on 245.

Notes   What we call the "back way" to Middleburg is the longer and hillier route that follows the original route along 626 about halfway to Middleburg before turning off on 628 and taking a more roundabout route to the town. It has significantly less traffic, but is 3.5 miles longer and has 500 feet more climbing. Some of our rides use the "original" way—THE PLAINS outbound, HORSE HILLS (long version) both ways, and the returning section BACKWARDS PLAINS (long)—and others use the "back way"—this ride, SPECTACLE LOOP and NO PLAINS, NO GAINS all outbound, as well as THE GAINESVILLE 50 on the way back. We made each choice for a reason, but we will switch the way we use depending on desire (when the choice is at the beginning of the ride), or how tired we are (when the choice is on the return portion).

44. Spectacle Loop

Distance *mi*	44.1
Category	IV
Climbing *ft*	3647
Rel. climb *ft/mi*	82.7

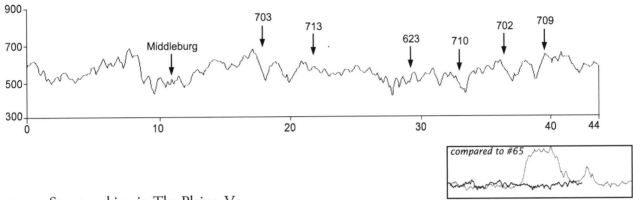

Start Street parking in The Plains, Va.

Route Starting from The Plains, this route takes the hillier back way into Middleburg. From there, it then goes up Middleburg hill and runs the ridge on Zulla Road to Frogtown Road. After passing through Rectortown, the route loops north on Rokeby Road, along 55 for a bit, then back south on Atoka Road. After heading back on Frogtown Road, the route returns to Zulla Road briefly, then angles toward The Plains on 707 and 704.

Notes This ride is one of our very favorites—featuring light traffic throughout, nicely rolling hills, and using the area north of Marshall and The Plains. If you are feeling strong early, the section beginning just after you turn onto 776 at mile seven provides a series of short but steep hills where you can get away from your group if you have the legs.

It seems that no ride from The Plains would be complete without using the oddly named but wonderful Frogtown Road. The area north of Marshall has three roads connecting Rectortown Road to Route 50: Atoka Road, Rokeby Road and Delaplane Grade Road. All three are so nice that we could ride them all day. This ride uses both Atoka and Rokeby—another reason we like this ride so much.

45. Picnic from The Plains

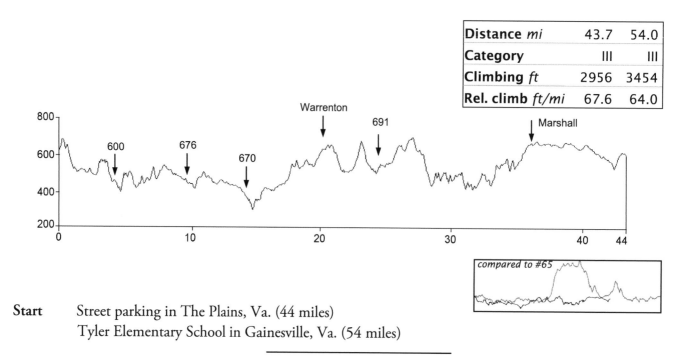

Distance *mi*	43.7	54.0
Category	III	III
Climbing *ft*	2956	3454
Rel. climb *ft/mi*	67.6	64.0

Start   Street parking in The Plains, Va. (44 miles)
Tyler Elementary School in Gainesville, Va. (54 miles)

Route   On the short version, the opening run along 55 tends downhill. Then the work begins on 600, which undulates along the Bull Run Mountains. The rollers continue on 670 on the approach to Warrenton, followed by the climb up to the city. Routes 678 and 691 continue the hills, but the ride finishes on the flat run from Marshall to The Plains. The long version starts from Gainesville, picks up the route at 600, circles around it, and then heads back to Gainesville. Bring your lunch and enjoy the rewards only a good ride can provide.

Notes   This route is a sampler of several other routes: SAMMY HAGAR, EAST OF WARRENTON, BLUE RIDGE VIEWS, and TALLY HO! Parts of it seem strange because they are not where they "should be." For example, the climb up to Middleburg is normally the last sprint battle of a ride on tired legs. Climbing it in the middle of a ride just doesn't feel right.

46. Backwards Plains

Distance *mi*	50.7	60.3
Category	III	III
Climbing *ft*	3471	4112
Rel. climb *ft/mi*	68.5	68.2

compared to #65

Start   Street parking in The Plains, Va.

Route   A relatively flat route for this region, this route begins by reversing the hallowed original THE PLAINS (#42) route to Marshall. In Marshall, it turns north on 710/Rectortown Road until 713/Atoka Road. It takes Atoka to 50 (briefly) and follows St. Louis Road to Snickersville Turnpike. After heading south on 719, a bit of zigzagging leads to Rokeby Road. The routes split after Frogtown Road, with the long route reversing the original Plains route by heading north on Zulla Road then south on 626. The shorter route tracks the closing miles of SPECTACLE LOOP (#44) back to The Plains.

Notes   St. Louis Road is excellent—great pavement and nice rolling hills—but this northern stretch of 734 has always been Scott's bane. The following section of 719 has hosted some vicious hill battles on its rollers. This is probably the hardest section of the ride as the profile shows. We often use this ride when century training time calls—usually in the late summer. The distance is great for building your endurance while the absence of any major climbs prevents the ride from totally draining your reserves.

For the profile of the final ten miles of the long route, see the opening ten miles of THE PLAINS (#42) in reverse.

47. Horse Hills

Distance *mi*	43.2	59.0
Category	IV	IV
Climbing *ft*	3322	4407
Rel. climb *ft/mi*	76.9	74.7

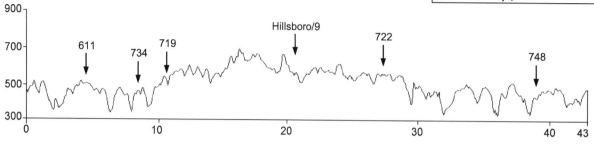

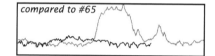

Start   Middleburg Elementary School in Middleburg, Va. (43 miles)
Street parking in The Plains, Va. (59 miles)

Route   The long version starts in The Plains, takes 626 to and from Middleburg where it joins the shorter version. For the profile of 626, see the opening eight miles of THE PLAINS (#42). The short version opens hard, climbing from the start. The rollers never really let up, but get easier as you warm up and several sections feature nice views and lightly trafficked roads. The stretch south of Hillsboro is a bit flatter than the rest of the ride, but the hills return as you near Middleburg.

Notes   We often neglect this ride, being too lazy to drive the extra eight miles to the Middleburg start point three seasons of the year. When we do take the extra time, we always are pleased by the sense of freshness from roads less frequently used.

For variety one fine day on this ride, Scott made the rules for a "green jersey" competition (like the Tour de France sprinter's jersey—don't we wish!). The first rule disallowed "off the front" attacks. Points only counted if everybody started together. This immediately neutralized young Michael's usual MO, which is to make everyone else chase on the roads leading to the big climbs, hopefully dulling Scott's advantage when it tilts up and just plain tiring Jim out. As Michael quickly realized, if the others did not chase his attack, he had to sit up or be disqualified for being too far ahead. This led him to declare that, "We shouldn't let lawyers make the rules," at least not rules that cut him out of the hunt!

A Chuck & Gail ride.

50. The Sammy Hagar Ride

Distance *mi*	39.4
Category	III
Climbing *ft*	2657
Rel. climb *ft/mi*	67.4

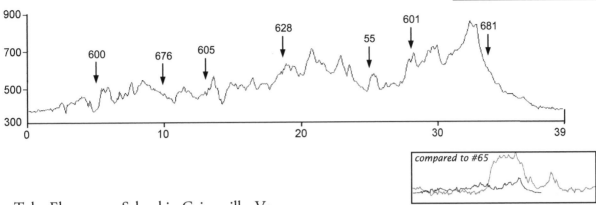

Start   Tyler Elementary School in Gainesville, Va.

Route   After the opening flat run on 55, 600 provides some hills as it runs along the shoulder of the Bull Run Mountains. As you near Warrenton, the section of 605 east of route 15 gets trafficky and has little shoulder. The stretch of 605 to the west of 15 is much better. After the return to Route 55, a couple of climbs lead to The Plains. Turning almost 180 degrees in The Plains, you parallel 55 on the rollers of Hopewell Road. Antioch Road tends downhill, so the last 5.5 miles are quickly ridden.

Notes   The first of our Gainesville rides, this one stays mostly south of 55. The turn onto 600 at just past mile five immediately challenges you with a steep ascent on a stair-step climb, but eventually levels out as you cruise down to the crossing of Route 15/29. The first miles on 605 are possibly our least favorite road anywhere. Once you cross 15, the traffic magically disappears and the 605/628 section back to 55 is one of the nicest roads to ride anywhere. The ride passes by the peaceful rural campus of the Airlie Foundation, a conference center built in the 1960s that includes a wildlife and habitat preservation project.

51. No Plains, No Gains

Distance *mi*	42.1
Category	IV
Climbing *ft*	3009
Rel. climb *ft/mi*	71.5

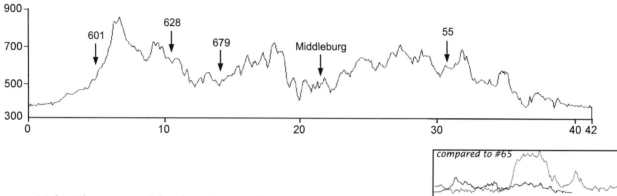

Start   Tyler Elementary School in Gainesville, Va.

Route   A little longer and a little hillier than THE SAMMY HAGAR RIDE (#50), this route stays north of 55 while SAMMY HAGAR stays mostly south. The opening flat stretch on 55 provides a warm-up before turning onto the predominantly uphill Antioch Road. The hills increase on Waterfall/Hopewell Road leading to The Plains. From there, you take the "back way" into Middleburg, which also has a few hills. From Middleburg, the ride goes up Middleburg hill then most of the way down Zulla Road. The route cuts off Zulla on 707 and 704, which are nicer and have less traffic. From there, it's a flat run back to Gainesville on 55.

Notes   Most of the hard hills come early in this ride. In Scott's opinion, once you reach the top of "Middleburg hill," the grade on rest of the ride is irrelevant: having battled up that hill for nearly a decade, nothing else matters if you reach the top first. Something about that hill incites us to "king of the mountain" battles more than any other climb.

For those who do care about the remaining pavement, Zulla Road has a fair amount of climbing, but most of it comes gradually. As you approach Haymarket, traffic on 55 increases, but the first few miles out of The Plains generally feature tolerable levels of traffic. Between Haymarket and Gainesville we suggest you ride single file for safety.

52. The Gainesville 50

Distance *mi*	49.6
Category	IV
Climbing *ft*	3843
Rel. climb *ft/mi*	77.5

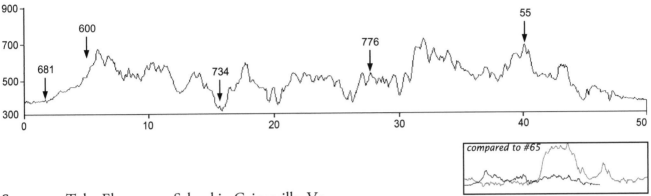

Start   Tyler Elementary School in Gainesville, Va.

Route   Beginning with the same five-and-a half-miles as NO PLAINS, NO GAINS (#51), this route then heads north on Mountain Road. Unusually for one of our rides, Mountain Road has a ¾-mile section of dirt. Neither of us enjoys dirt roads on a road bike, but the roads on the other side are so nice that the dirt is worth it. After a short stretch on 50, the route takes the lower end of Snickersville Turnpike, a lovely road with little traffic. Route 626 south to Middleburg has some rollers, but the real climbs on this ride are on 776. After reversing this "back way to Middleburg," the route finishes on 55.

Notes   Depending on the weather, we start this ride two different ways. Mountain Road has the stretch of dirt in the first couple of miles, so if the roads are wet we prefer the alternate start, which avoids the mud at the expense of traffic.

Although this ride starts from one of our main start points, much of the opening half of the ride is spent on roads unique to this ride. The stretch from the beginning of Mountain Road to 50 is particularly nice (except for the dirt), featuring very light traffic paired with dense trees.

60. Tally Ho!

Distance *mi*	37.9	50.0
Category	IV	IV
Climbing *ft*	3205	3720
Rel. climb *ft/mi*	84.6	74.4

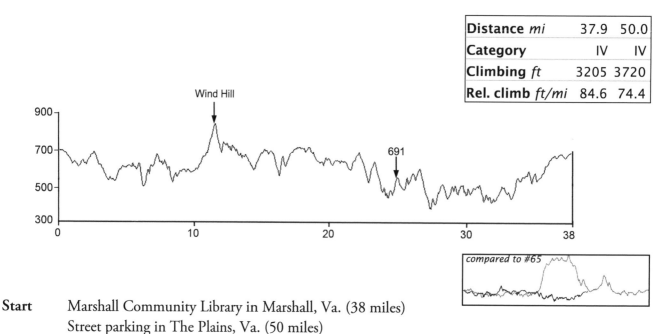

Start   Marshall Community Library in Marshall, Va. (38 miles)
Street parking in The Plains, Va. (50 miles)

Route   Opening with an easy ten miles, the rest of the ride is something altogether different. From Marshall, the route zigzags across I-66 to Markham. The route then turns south on 688 and ascends Wind Hill as the first of many climbs. In Hume you turn east along 635. After skirting Big Cobbler Mountain, you continue south on 647 and 738. Almost at Warrenton, you turn north on 691 and rise and fall back to Marshall. The long version starts in The Plains. See the first six-and-a-half miles of the profile of BACKWARDS PLAINS (#46) for the long version addition.

Notes   The area south of I-66 and bracketed by Front Royal on the west and Marshall on the east seems to be entirely carpeted with rolling hills. The big climbs (Naked Mountain and Mt. Weather) are to the north and Chester Gap is almost at the western edge. Despite the lack of a major climb in this area, moments on flat roads are few and far between. The first spring ride in these hills is often both painful and humbling, as you wonder where all that strength you had a few short months ago disappeared to! As spring hazes into summer, we tend to want longer rides and the alternate start in The Plains provides one. Don't let the hills dissuade you—this region has its own distinct beauty.

Mostly a Chuck & Gail ride.

61. Bug, Sweat & Tears

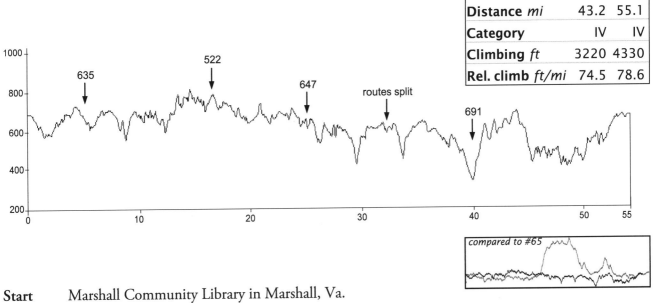

Distance *mi*	43.2	55.1
Category	IV	IV
Climbing *ft*	3220	4330
Rel. climb *ft/mi*	74.5	78.6

compared to #65

Start   Marshall Community Library in Marshall, Va.

Route   Starting from Marshall, the route follows 55 for less than a mile before turning south on 647. The hills begin in earnest at mile 5.5, when the route turns west on 635. Big Cobbler Mountain looms ahead, but the route skirts the base. At 522, the route turns south for three miles then takes a brief respite from the hills with a small loop west of 522. The short route takes 647 back almost to Marshall, while the long route bends south on 688 and heads north to Marshall on 691, taking in that road's many rollers.

Notes   This ride is the toughest of our category IV rides. Despite staying mostly between 500 and 800 feet of elevation, the route features a lot of climbing. 635 has plenty of rollers to keep your legs burning. The relatively flat stretch west of 522 provides a welcome break from the rollers, which return on 647.

Watch out for the bugs in the springtime—Jim has consumed more than his share on this ride! Despite that, this ride has always been one of his favorites, probably because the second half suits his abilities so well—a steady diet of rollers, most of which you can power over if you're in shape.

62. The Marshall Plan

Distance *mi*		39.4
Category		III
Climbing *ft*		2792
Rel. climb *ft/mi*		70.9

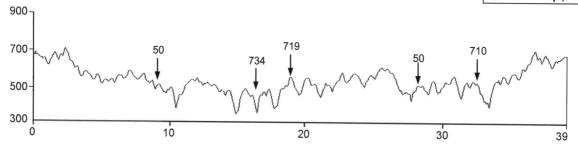

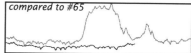

compared to #65

Start   Marshall Community Library in Marshall, Va.

Route   This ride is a shortened and modified version of BACKWARDS PLAINS (#46), starting and ending in Marshall instead of The Plains. A relatively flat route for this region, this ride begins heading north on Rectortown Road until Atoka Road. It takes Atoka to 50 (briefly) and follows St. Louis Road to Snickersville Turnpike. In Airmont, the route turns south on 719. A bit of zigzagging leads to Rokeby Road. It finishes by reversing the opening seven miles of Rectortown Road.

Notes   St. Louis Road is one of the better roads in the area. Although not as lightly trafficked nor as picturesque as many others, it has great pavement and nice rolling hills that are enjoyable in either direction—BULLS ON PARADE (#43) traverses St. Louis Road in the other direction and we enjoy it just as much. In contrast, the last five miles of Rectortown Road are unusual because they are difficult in either direction: southbound because those five miles are at the end of a ride when you are tired and the hills hurt all the more; northbound because those miles are at the beginning of a ride when we are usually struggling to hold the wheel of our friend Michael, a very fast starter.

This ride is an excellent either as an introduction to the Marshall region or as an off-season ride: it's neither too long nor too hilly and provides a nice change of scenery from similar rides in Montgomery County.

63. Stormin' the Gap

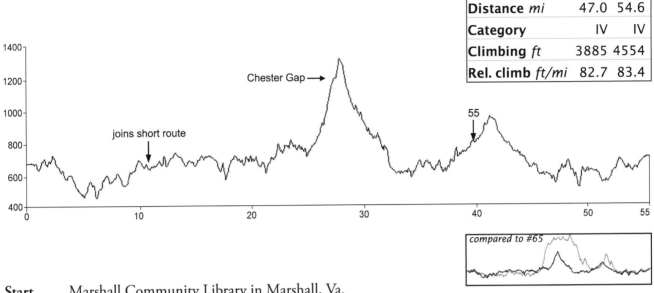

Distance *mi*	47.0	54.6
Category	IV	IV
Climbing *ft*	3885	4554
Rel. climb *ft/mi*	82.7	83.4

Start Marshall Community Library in Marshall, Va.

Route Starting from Marshall, the long version loops up Rectortown Road and back down 713 to add a little over seven miles to the shorter route, if desired. The short version starts by heading west on 55 from Marshall. The routes meet up at 732, which heads south to our main east-west road in his region, 635. After many rollers, the route T's at 522. Where BUG, SWEAT & TEARS (#61) turns south at this point, this route heads north and climbs Chester Gap. A long descent drops you into Front Royal. Traffic can be heavy on Happy Creek Road (624), but that is generally the only traffic seen. The route eventually joins up with Route 55, which features generally light traffic eastbound.

Notes Hope for a westerly wind for this ride: you won't notice the headwind outbound when battling the rollers on 635, but you'll love it on the return leg as it will carry you back to Marshall.

As with most of the Marshall rides, one climb defines the ride. On this ride, that climb is Chester Gap. At the end of 635, you come to a stop, make a right turn and then it is a straight shot up and over into Front Royal. If you are feeling strong, try going hard from the gun, pushing to the top, and then attacking the descent, which seems twice as long as the climb. There are no turns to worry about, so nobody can get lost if you are riding with a group. It's a straight power contest.

Chester Gap has been one of Jim's favorite climbs ever since he won the polka dot jersey on our inaugural ride up it. Scott evened the score on the second ride, but the first victory is always the sweetest.

64. Piedmont Pig Ride

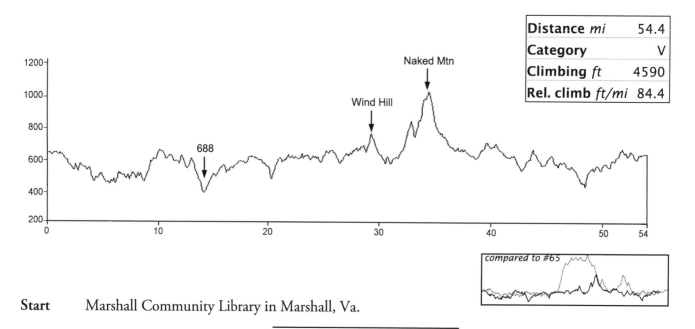

Distance *mi*	54.4
Category	V
Climbing *ft*	4590
Rel. climb *ft/mi*	84.4

Start Marshall Community Library in Marshall, Va.

Route The first eight miles are relatively easy, running south on 691. Then the fun begins, as the south end of 691 and most of 688 feature several good climbs. As you approach 55, 688 offers up one last climb up Wind Hill. North of 55, the route climbs Naked Mountain from the south. The grade goes double-digit briefly. You bleed off 800 feet of the hard won elevation over the next 14 miles, as you take 17, then 55, then Delaplane Grade Road back toward Rectortown. The ride finishes with the small rollers on Rectortown Road.

Notes Save this ride for a day you really want to be challenged and reserve your spot on the couch for the post-ride recovery! Don't be fooled by the easy first nine miles—the climb after the turn at mile 9.6 will put a significant dent in your average speed. Looking at the profile of the last six miles makes it clear why this stretch always seems so hard—not only does it come at the end of the ride when your legs are tired, but it tends uphill. Look for the ride's namesake in the field just before 757 at the bottom of Wind Hill.

65. The Blue Ridger

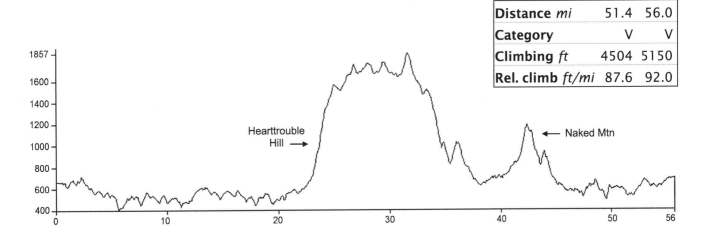

Distance *mi*	51.4	56.0
Category	V	V
Climbing *ft*	4504	5150
Rel. climb *ft/mi*	87.6	92.0

Start   Marshall Community Library in Marshall, Va.

Route   The ride begins by heading north from Marshall on relatively flat roads. North of 50, the section on 719 is always nice. The stretch on Snickersville Turnpike is where the fear begins to set in. The very end of 734 features a nasty but brief climb. A quick stretch on 7, also uphill, takes you to the base of Hearttrouble Hill. From the base, the view is nothing but hill, as far as the eye can see. Once at the "top," the ridge is rolling to Mt. Weather. The descent is fun, and the store at the intersection of 17 and 601 (sadly no longer open) is a good place to regroup.

The routes split soon after this intersection. The classic long route heads south, eventually turning off on 688 for the second climb near Naked Mountain. As bad as that climb might seem, it is harder from the other side (see #64, PIEDMONT PIG RIDE). The long route closes with another relatively flat run paralleling I-66 back to Marshall. The shorter route skips the Naked Mountain climb and returns to Marshal by the same route as the closing miles of ride #64.

Notes   This is one of our most challenging rides and probably the best-known ride of Chuck and Gail's. The ride is defined by the two major climbs. The other climbs, which would be noticeable on any other ride, shrink to almost nothing by comparison. Although very challenging, the sense of accomplishment upon finishing is great. Be sure to come with appropriate gearing!

The first time Michael rode this ride he was a novice and had just bought a used 7-speed with a 53/42 chainring combination and a 21-tooth large cog in the back. Not knowing what was to come, his first comment after reaching the other side was, "I'm going to get a 39-tooth ring."

Still, no gearing combination has ever allowed anyone to stay within shouting distance of Scott on a good day (and shouts go far on a mountain), and he always has a good day on the big climbs. We can each take him on some of the climbs in the category III and IV rides, but his prowess on the big climbs reminds us why his name comes first on the book.

Mostly a Chuck & Gail ride.

40. Lovetts or Lees It

Distance:	43 miles	
Rating:	III	
Start:	Loudoun County High School in Leesburg, Va.	

0.0	R	699, Dry Mill Rd from parking (to head west)
3.5	R	9 at top of hill
4.2	R	662, Clarke's Gap Rd
6.6	S	665, High St in **Waterford**. Becomes Butcher's Row, then Loyalty Rd
12.4	L	663, Taylorstown Rd in **Taylorstown**. B/c 668
14.5	L	672, Lovettsville Rd at T. Becomes 673, E Broadway in **Lovettsville**
18.0	S	673, W Broadway at 287. Becomes Irish Corner Rd
20.4	BR	690, Mountain Rd
24.3	R	690, Mountain Rd at 693, Morrisonville Rd
27.5	R	9, Charlestown Pike at T
27.6	L	690, Hillsboro Rd
30.6	L	711, Allder School Rd
31.9	R	611, Purcellville Rd at SS
33.3	L	onto W&OD
39.6	L	699, Dry Mill Rd at T
43.1	L	to parking

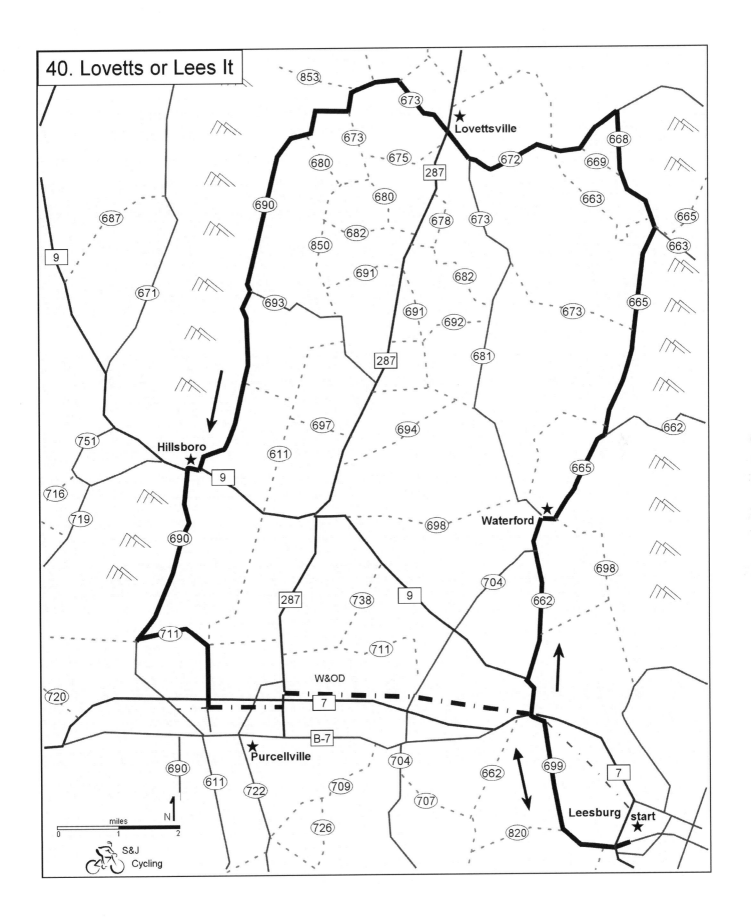

40. Lovetts or Lees It

853

673

Lovettsville

673

675

672

668

680

287

669

690

687

680

663

665

9

682

678

673

663

850

671

691

682

665

693

691

692

673

287

681

751

697

694

Hillsboro

611

665

9

716

Waterford

690

698

719

662

698

711

704

720

W&OD

738

711

9

7

662

290

611

722

B-7

704

Purcellville

709

704

662

699

7

726

707

Leesburg   start

820

miles

N

S&J
Cycling

121

42. The Plains

Distance:	**34** or 39 miles
Rating:	III
Start:	Street parking in The Plains, Va.

34 Mile Ride

0.1	L	626, Loudoun Ave at T from parking road	22.5	L	F185 just before 17/55. B/c 55
			☞ *		
8.0	L	50, Washington St in **Middleburg**	29.2	R	709
9.2	L	709, Zulla Rd	30.2	L	750
14.1	R	702, Frogtown Rd	31.8	L	245 at T
17.5	R	710, Rectortown Rd at T	33.5	R	55 at T in **The Plains**
☜ *			33.6	L	626, Loudoun Ave
18.9	L	713 in **Rectortown**	33.7	L	804 at RR tracks to parking

*39 Mile Ride

18.9	S	710, Rectortown Rd	27.7	L	713
22.8	L	712, Delaplane Grade Rd	27.8	R	F185. B/c 55
26.5	L	17 ☹			

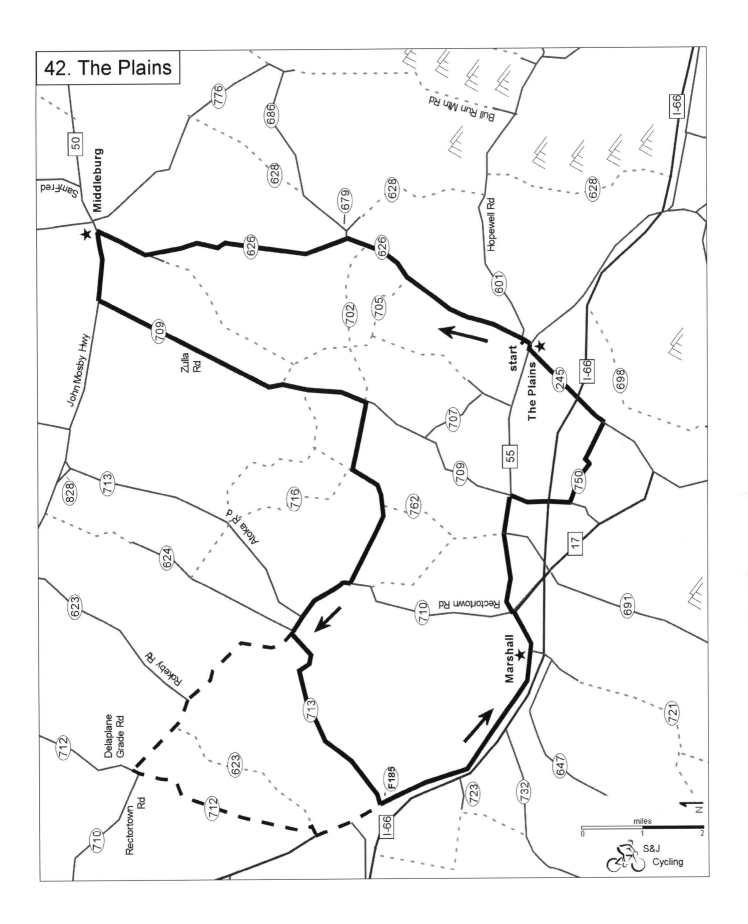

42. The Plains

43. Bulls on Parade

Distance:	35 or **38** miles
Rating:	IV
Start:	Street parking in The Plains, Va.

38 Mile Ride

0.0	L	626, Loudoun Ave at T from parking road
3.6	R	679, Landmark Rd. Becomes 628
4.8	S	686
7.0	BL	629
7.2	L	776
11.4	S	626, Pot House Rd, crossing 50 at light in **Middleburg**
16.4	L	611, St. Louis Rd at SS
20.2	R	50 at T ☹
20.7	L	713 (first left)
20.8	BL	713, Atoka Rd
25.9	L	710 at T
27.0	L	702, Frogtown Rd
30.4	R	709, Zulla Rd ☞ *
33.2	S	709, crossing 55
34.2	L	750
35.8	L	245 (unmarked) at T
37.5	R	55 at T in **The Plains**
37.6	L	626, Loudoun Ave
37.7	L	804, Stuart St at RR tracks (to parking road)

*35 Mile Ride

31.8	L	707
33.1	BR	704
33.7	L	55 at T
34.8	L	626 in **The Plains**
34.9	L	804, Stuart St. at RR tracks (to parking road)

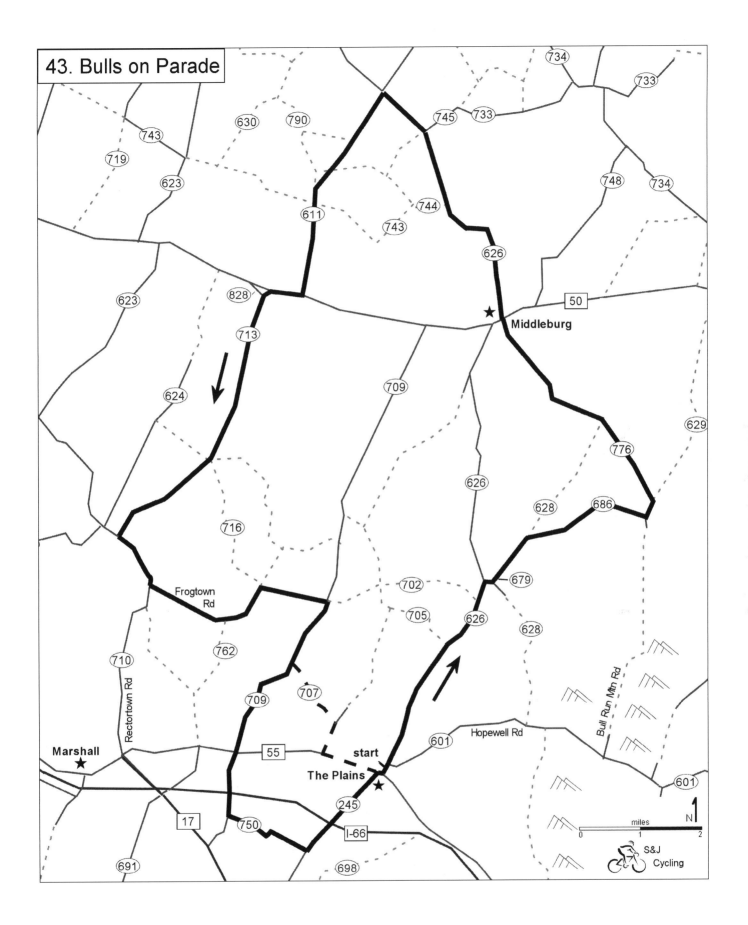

43. Bulls on Parade

125

44. The Spectacle Loop

Distance:	**44** miles	
Rating:	IV	
Start:	Street parking in The Plains, Va.	

0.0	L	626, Loudoun Ave at T from parking road		29.9	R	828, Rector's Lane
3.6	R	679, Landmark Rd. Becomes 628		30.3	R	713, Atoka Rd
4.8	S	686		35.3	L	710 at T
7.0	BL	629		36.3	L	702, Frogtown Rd
7.2	L	776. Becomes South Madison St in **Middleburg**		39.9	R	709, Zulla Rd
11.4	L	50 at light		41.1	L	707, Milestone Rd
12.8	L	709, Zulla Rd		42.3	BR	704
17.6	R	702, Frogtown Rd		42.9	L	55
21.1	R	710 at T		43.9	L	626, Loudoun Ave in **The Plains**
24.7	R	623, Rokeby Rd		44.1	L	804 at RR tracks (to parking road)
28.3	R	50 ☹				

44. Spectacle Loop

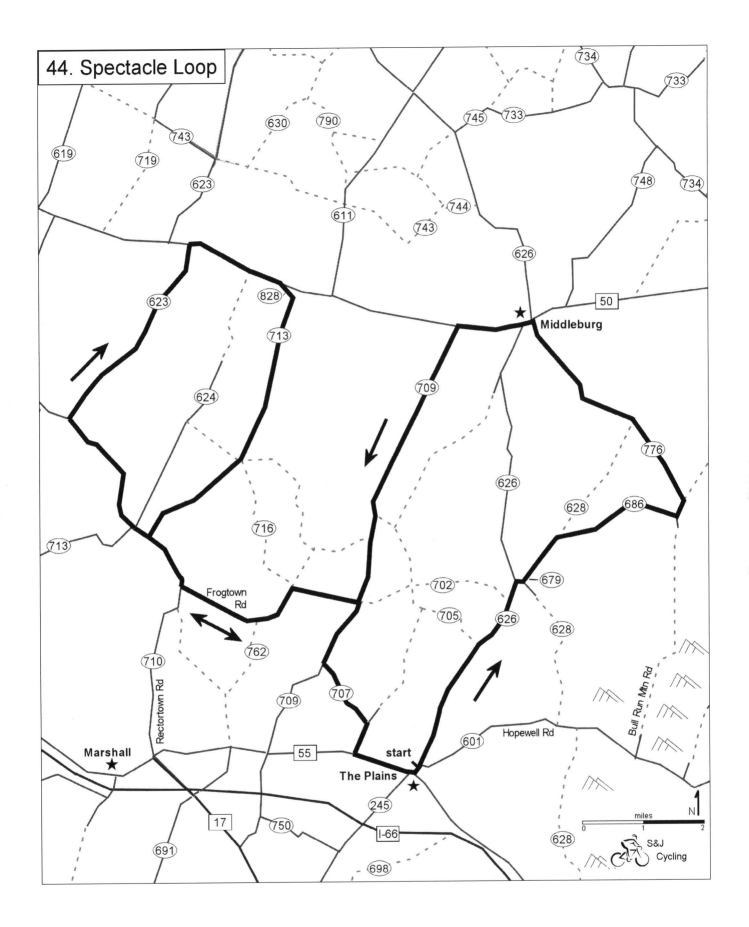

45. Picnic from the Plains

Distance:	44 or 54 miles
Rating:	III
Start:	Street parking in The Plains, Va. (44 miles) or
	Tyler Elementary School in Gainesville, Va. (54 miles)

44 Mile Ride (The Plains)

0.0	R	626, Loudoun Ave at T from parking road	22.0	L	Waterloo Rd at SS, becomes 678
0.2	L	55 ☞*	25.9	BR	691/678, becomes 691
4.8	R	600 (cross 15/29 at light at mile 8.9)	28.3	R	691 (on downhill)
			36.7	L	17 ☹
10.1	R	676	37.4	R	1001 in **Marshall** (store)
12.5	L	605 at T			
13.8	R	602, Rogues Rd	37.6	R	55
14.8	R	670 at SS	39.3	R	709
14.9	R	670 at 602 at T after bridge	40.3	L	750
19.2	R	643 at SS	41.7	L	245
20.6	S	Lee St at SS in **Warrenton**	43.5	R	55 in **The Plains** ☞*
21.1	R	Ashby St	43.6	L	626, Loudoun Ave
21.2	L	Waterloo St at SS	43.7	L	804 at RR tracks to parking
21.9	S	211 at light			
22.0	R	Rappahannock St			

*54 Mile Ride** (Gainesville)

0.0	L	west on 55 from parking	43.6	S	55 at 626 in **The Plains**
5.2	L	600 (to main ride) *****	54.0	R	to parking in **Gainesville**

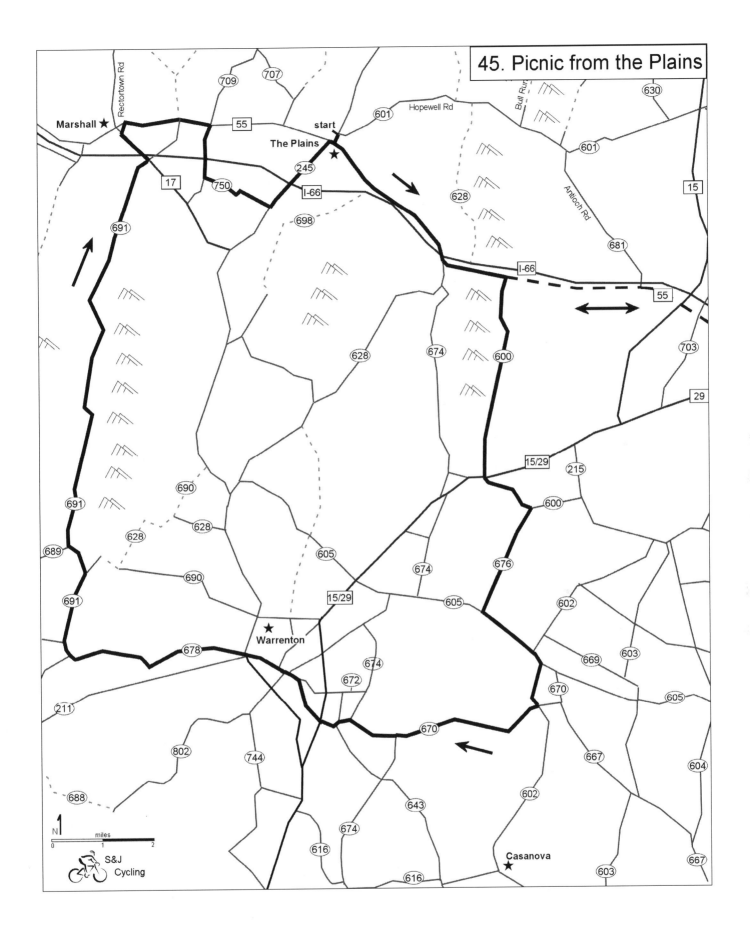

45. Picnic from the Plains

Marshall

The Plains

start

Hopewell Rd

Warrenton

Casanova

S&J
Cycling

N

miles
0   1   2

46. Backwards Plains

Distance:	51 or 60 miles
Rating:	III
Start:	Street parking in The Plains, Va.

51 Mile Ride

0.0	R	626, Loudoun Ave at T from parking road
0.1	R	55
0.2	L	245
1.9	R	750
3.5	R	709 at T
4.5	L	55
6.4	R	710, Rectortown Rd at SL in **Marshall**
10.5	R	713, Atoka Rd
15.4	BR	TRO 713, Atoka Rd
15.5	R	50 ☹
16.2	L	611, St. Louis Rd
23.4	L	734, Snickersville Turnpike
25.9	L	719, Airmont Rd. B/c Green Garden Rd

32.5	L	743, Milville Rd
33.7	BR	623
35.3	L	50
35.6	R	623, Rokeby Rd
39.2	L	710, Rectortown Rd
43.0	L	702, Frogtown Rd ☞ *
46.3	R	709, Zulla Rd
47.5	L	707, Milestone Rd
48.9	BR	704
49.5	L	55 at T
50.6	L	626 in **The Plains**
50.7	L	804, Stuart St at RR tracks (to parking road)

*60 Mile Ride

46.3	L	709, Zulla Rd
51.2	R	50

52.4	R	626
60.3	R	804 at RR tracks (to parking road) in **The Plains**

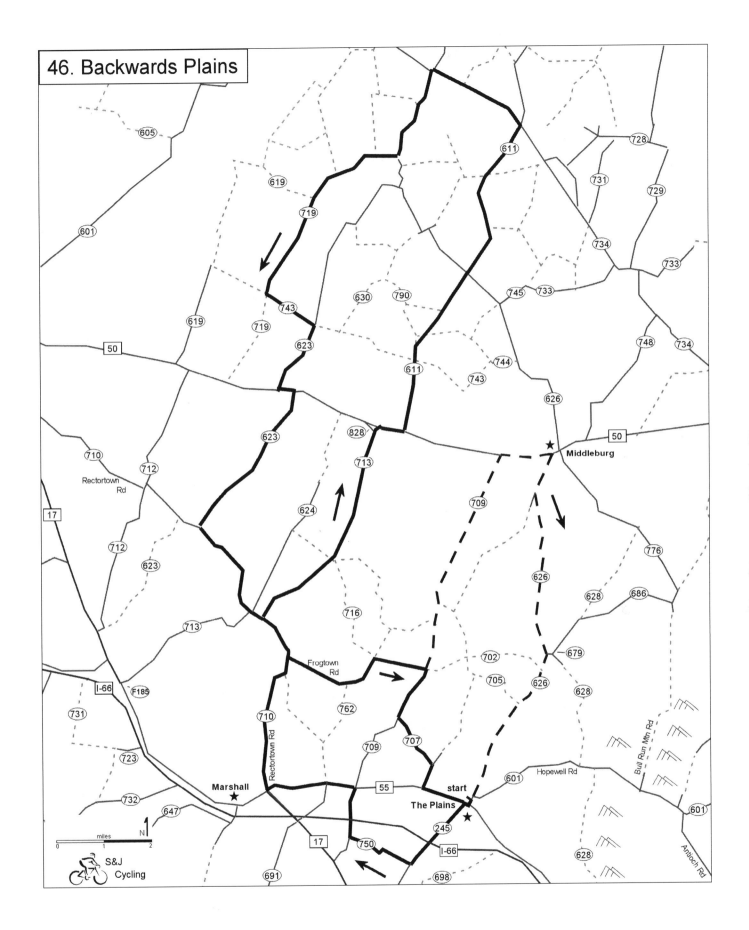

46. Backwards Plains

605
728
619
731
729
611
601
619
719
734
733
743
630
790
745
733
50
719
748
734
623
744
611
743
623
828
626
713
50
710
Middleburg
712
624
709
Rectortown Rd
17
776
712
623
628
686
716
679
713
702
Frogtown Rd
626
628
I-66 F185
762
705
731
710
709 707
723
601 Hopewell Rd
Marshall
55
start
732
The Plains
647
245
17
I-66
601
750
628
691
698

N
miles
0   1   2

S&J
Cycling

47. Horse Hills

Distance:	**43** or 59 miles
Rating:	IV
Start:	Middleburg Elementary School in Middleburg, Va. (43 miles)
	Street parking in The Plains, Va. (59 miles)

43 Mile Ride

0.0 ☞ *	R	626, Foxcroft Rd from pkg
4.8	R	611, St Louis Rd
8.6	L	734, Snickersville Tpke
11.0	R	719, Airmont Rd in **Airmont** (store)
14.6	S	719, Woodgrove Rd at Bus 7 in **Round Hill**
19.5	R	719, Stony Point Rd at 751, Cider Mill Rd
20.8	R	9 at T in **Hillsboro** ☹
21.1	R	812
21.3	L	812, Gaver Mill Rd at 718
21.6	R	690, Hillsboro Rd at T
24.3	L	711, Allder School Rd
25.6	R	611, Purcellville Rd at SS, b/c Hatcher Ave in **Purcellville**
27.1	L	Bus 7, Main St at T
27.6	R	722, S Maple Ave. Becomes Lincoln Rd
33.2	R	728, North Fork Rd at T
33.9	L	731, Water Mill Rd
36.1	L	734, Snickersville Tpke at T
38.9	R	748, Sam Fred Rd
42.3 ☞ **	R	50, John Mosby Hwy at SS (mile 50.5 of long route)
42.8	R	Jay St in **Middleburg**
42.9	L	T1202, Marshall St
43.1	R	626 at SS
43.2	R	to parking

*59 Mile Ride, part 1

0.1	L	626, Loudoun Ave at T from parking road
8.0	R	50, Washington St in **Middleburg**
8.1	L	626, Madison St Join 43-mi ride at school

**59 Mile Ride, part 2

51.1	L	626 in **Middleburg**
59.0	R	804 at RR tracks to parking

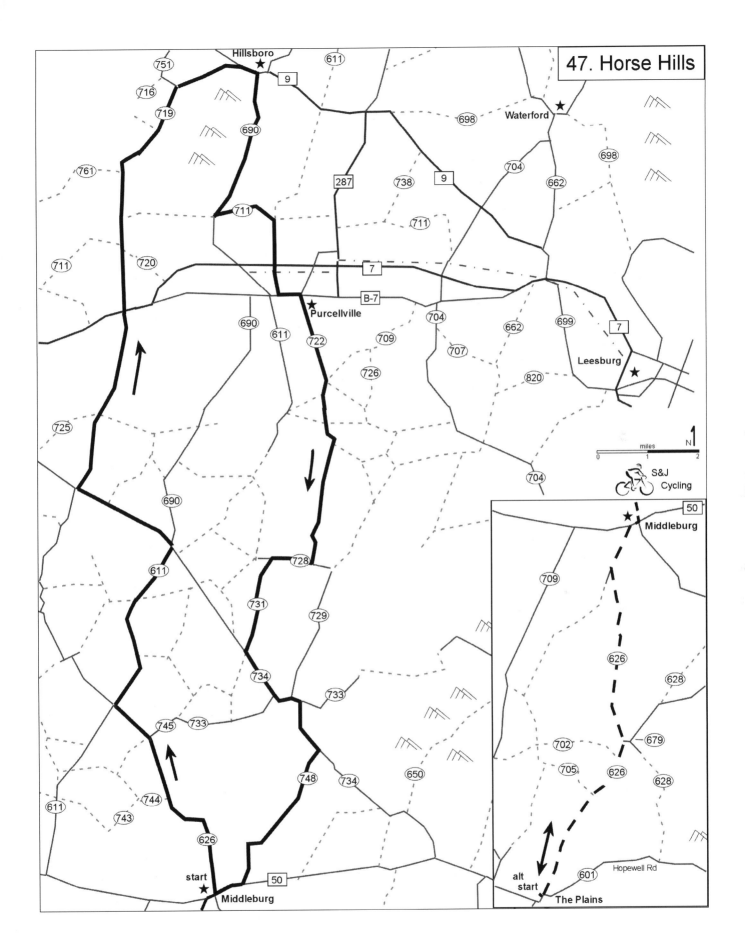

47. Horse Hills

50. The Sammy Hagar Ride

Distance:	39 miles	
Rating:	III	
Start:	Tyler Elementary School in Gainesville, Va.	

0.1	R	55 from parking
5.2	L	600, Beverlys Mill Rd
9.3	X	15/29 at light
10.4	R	676
12.7	R	605 at T ☹
15.4	X	15/29 TRO 605 at light
18.7	R	628, Blantyre Rd at T

24.8	BL	674
25.2	L	55
28.5	R	626 in **The Plains**
28.7	R	601, Hopewell Rd after tracks
33.9	R	681, Antioch Rd
37.1	L	55 at T
39.4	L	to parking

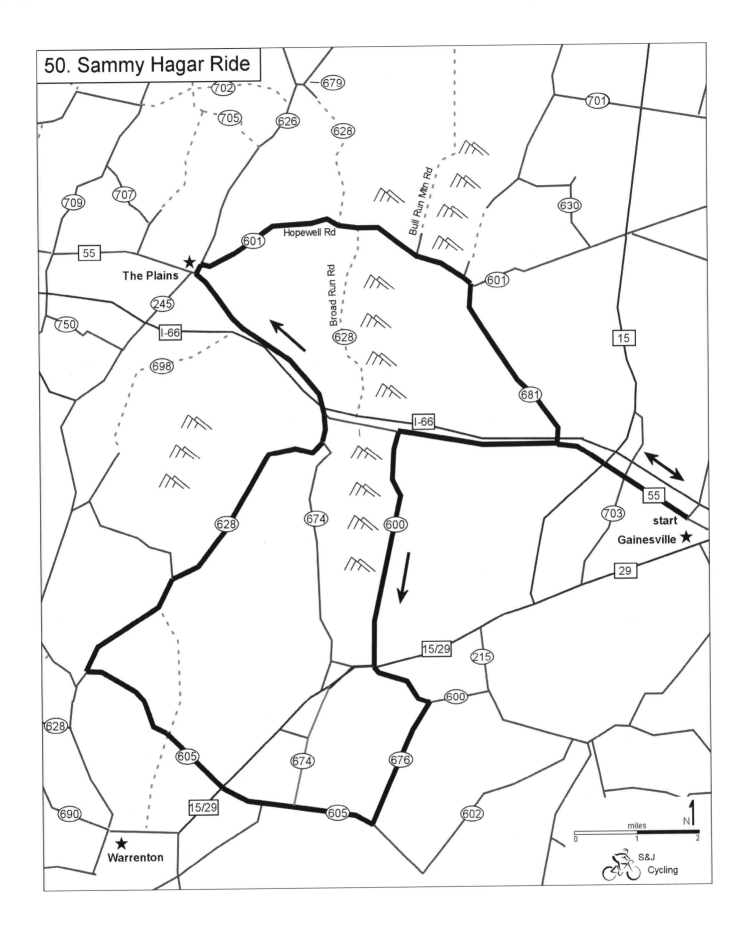

50. Sammy Hagar Ride

679
702
705
626
628
701
709
707
630
601 Hopewell Rd
55
Bull Run Mtn Rd
The Plains
245
601
750
I-66
15
698
Broad Run Rd
628
I-66
681
628
674
600
703
start
Gainesville
29
15/29
215
628
600
605
674
676
690
15/29
605
602
628
Warrenton

miles
0   1   2
N

S&J
Cycling

51. No Plains, No Gains

Distance:	42 miles	
Rating:	IV	
Start:	Tyler Elementary School in Gainesville, Va.	

0.1	R	55 from school
2.3	R	681, Antioch Rd
5.5	L	601, Waterfall Rd at T
10.7	R	626, Loudoun Ave at T
14.3	R	679, Landmark Rd. Becomes 628
15.5	S	686
17.7	BL	629, Bull Run Mtn Rd
17.9	L	776, Landmark School Rd. Becomes South Madison St in **Middleburg**
22.1	L	50 at light
23.5	L	709, Zulla Rd
29.6	L	707, Milestone Rd
30.8	BR	704
31.4	L	55
42.1	L	to school

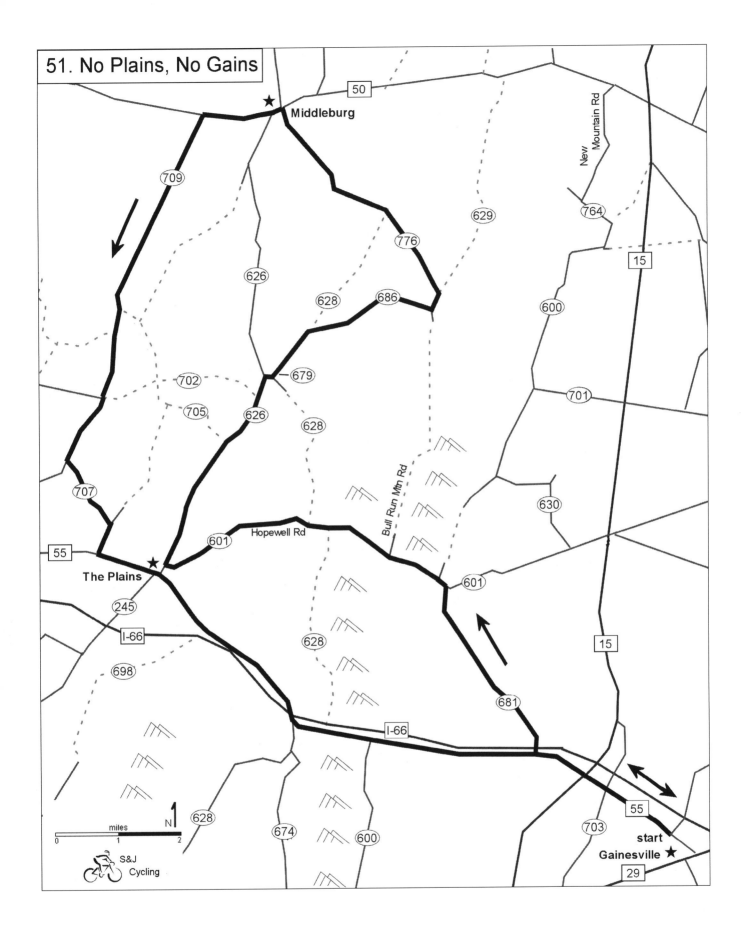

51. No Plains, No Gains

52. The Gainesville 50

Distance:	50 miles
Rating:	IV
Start:	Tyler Elementary School in Gainesville, Va.

50 Mile Ride

0.1 ☞*	R	55 from school		24.7	L	626, Foxcroft Rd, becomes N Madison St
2.3	R	681, Antioch Rd		28.5	R	W Marshall St
5.5	L	601, Waterfall Rd at T (unpaved)		28.5	L	N Madison St
5.7 ☞*	R	600, Mountain Rd (unpaved for 0.75 mi)		28.6	S	S Madison St in **Middleburg**. Becomes 776, Landmark School Rd.
12.2	L	615, Loudoun Dr		32.9	R	629, Bull Run Mtn Rd
12.7	L	764, Buchanon Gap Rd		33.1	R	686. Becomes 628. Becomes 679, Landmark Rd
13.4	R	631, New Mountain Rd				
15.4	L	50 ☹		36.3	L	626, Halfway Rd at T
16.5	R	734, Snickersville Tpke		39.7	L	55
21.1	BL	TRO 734		49.4	L	to school
21.7	L	733, Mountville Rd				
24.0	BL	745				

*No Dirt Route (0.2 miles longer)

1.0	R	625, Jefferson St (before 15), b/c Old Carolina Rd		5.8	R	630, Mill Creek Rd
2.2	R	15 ☹		7.1	L	2010, Berkeley Dr
5.2	L	601, Waterfall Rd		8.0	R	600, Mountain Rd to rejoin other route (next turn is in 4.4 miles on 615)

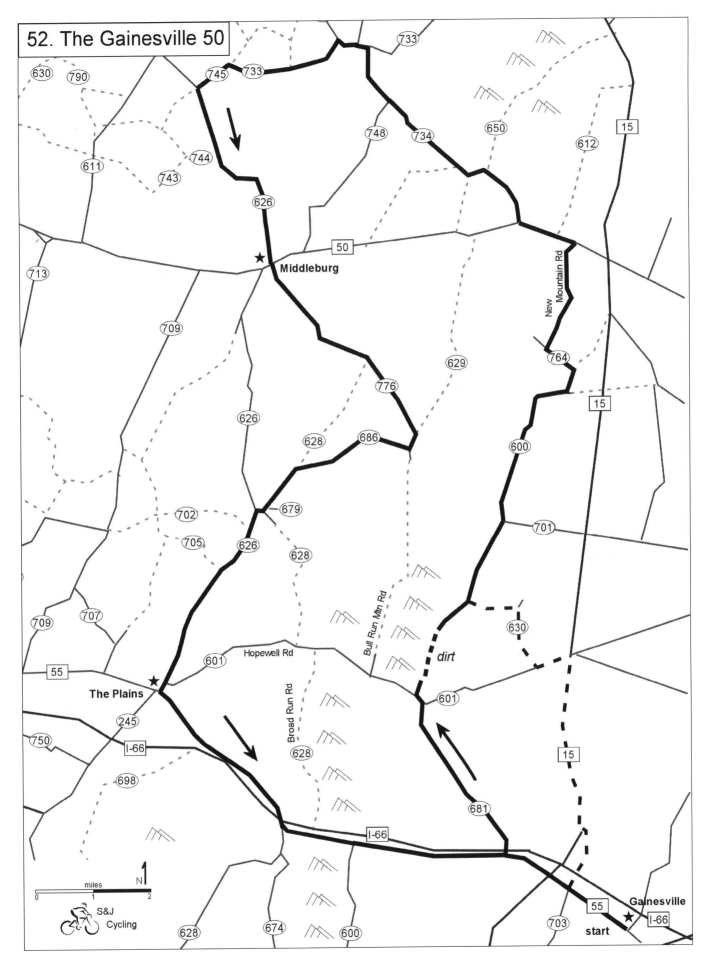

52. The Gainesville 50

630 790

745 733 733

630

744

743 611

626

713

Middleburg 50

709

709 707

702 705

626

626

628

679

628

55

601 Hopewell Rd

The Plains

245

750

I-66

698

628

Broad Run Rd

628

Bull Run Mtn Rd

674

600

748

734

650

612

15

629

776

686

764

New Mountain Rd

600

15

701

630

dirt

601

681

15

703

55

Gainesville

start I-66

miles

0 1 2

N

S&J Cycling

60. Tally Ho!

Distance:	**38** or 50 miles
Rating:	IV
Start:	Marshall Community Center in Marshall, Va. (38 miles) or The Plains Library in The Plains, Va. (50 miles)

38 Mile Ride

0.0	L	710, Rectortown Rd from parking		19.5	R	647 at SS
0.1	R	55, Main St at SL. B/c F185 ☞ *		20.9	L	733
				21.6	S	738
3.3	L	723, crossing I-66		27.2	S	689
3.4	R	F184, immediately after crossing I-66		27.9	L	691
5.4	R	731 at SS		36.6	L	17 at T ☹ (mile 42.9 of long route) ☞ *
5.5	L	55 after crossing under I-66		37.8	S	710, Rectortown Rd at SS in **Marshall**
9.4	L	757 in **Markham**. B/c 688				
15.3	L	635 in **Hume** (store)		37.9	R	to parking

*50 Mile Ride

0.0	R	626, Loudoun Ave at T from parking road		43.6	R	1001 in **Marshall** (store)
0.1	R	55		43.8	R	55
0.2	L	245		45.5	R	709
1.9	R	750		46.5	L	750
3.5	R	709 at T		47.9	L	245
4.5	L	55		49.7	R	55 in **The Plains**
6.4	S	55 at 710, Rectortown Rd in **Marshall** to join 38-mi ride		49.8	L	626, Loudoun Ave
* * * * *				49.9	L	804 at RR tracks to parking

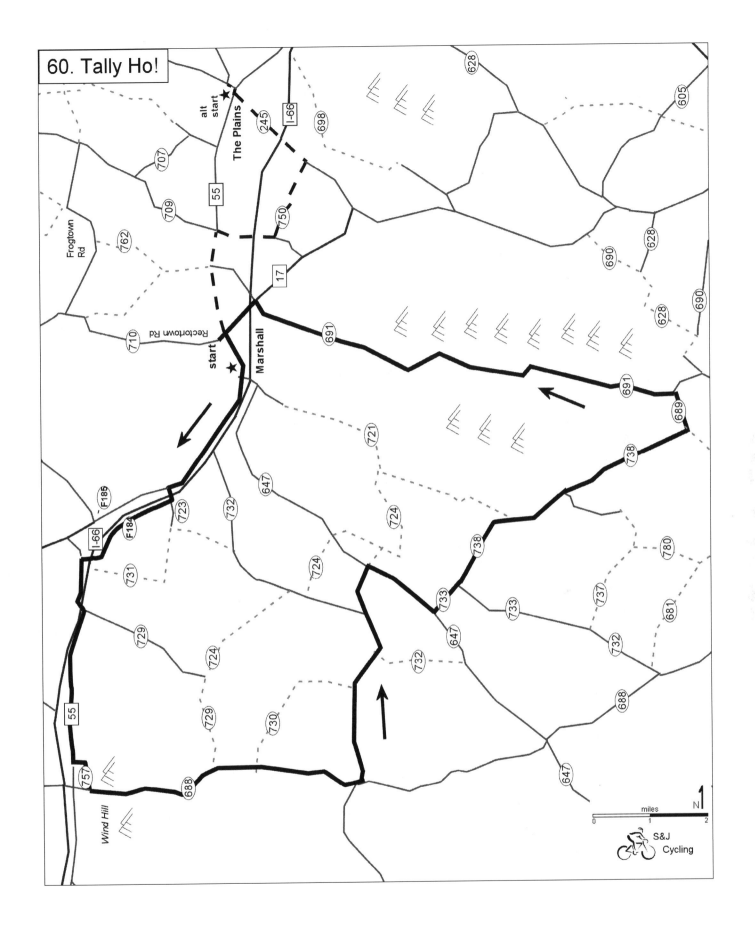

60. Tally Ho!

61. Bug, Sweat & Tears

Distance:	43 or **55** miles
Rating:	IV
Start:	Marshall Community Library in Marshall, Va.

55 Mile Ride

0.0	L	710 from parking
0.1	R	Main St at SL
0.8	L	647
1.1	R	647 after passing over I-66
5.5	R	635
17.0	L	522 at T ☹
20.1	R	630
20.9	BL	628
23.0	BL	628
23.7	L	606
25.1	L	522 in **Flint Hill** (stores)

25.3 ☞*	R	647
33.0	R	688, Leeds Manor Rd
35.4		**Orlean** (store)
41.0	L	691 in **Waterloo**
43.1	L	691
44.9	BL	691
45.5	R	691, Carter's Run Rd
53.9	L	17 ☹
55.0	S	710, crossing Main St in **Marshall**
55.1	R	into parking

*43 Mile Ride

33.0	S	647
42.3	L	647

42.6	R	55/17
43.2	L	710 to parking

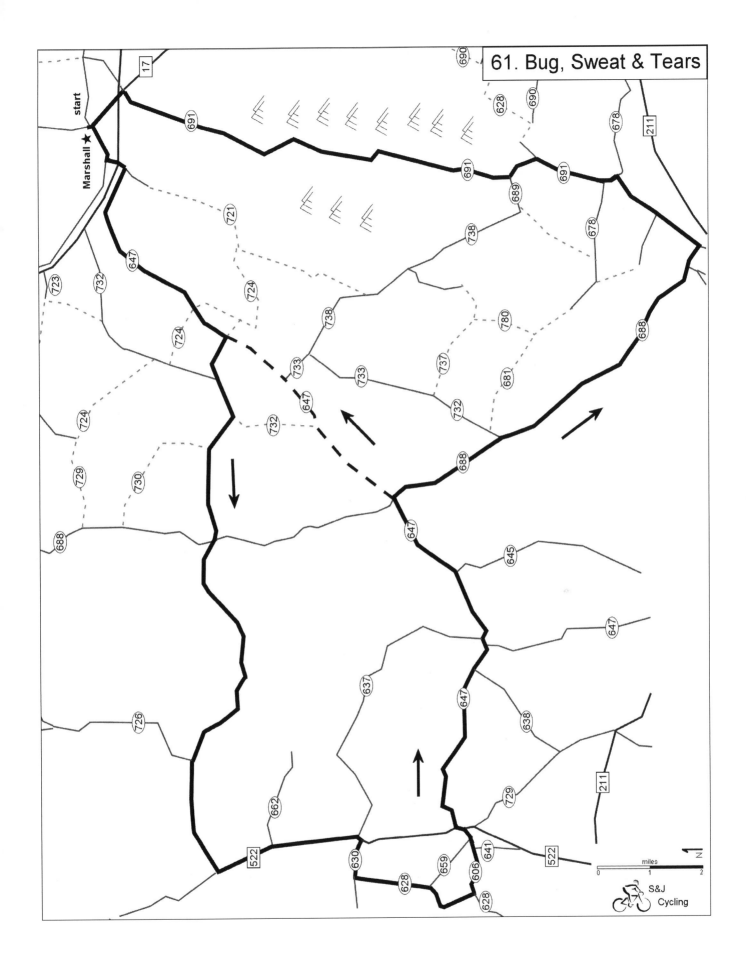

61. Bug, Sweat & Tears

62. The Marshall Plan

Distance:	39 miles	
Rating:	II	
Start:	Marshall Community Library in Marshall, Va.	

0.0	R	710, Rectortown Rd from parking in **Marshall**	19.4	L	719, Airmont Rd B/c Green Garden Rd
4.0	R	713, Atoka Rd	26.0	L	743, Milville Rd
8.9	BR	TRO 713, Atoka Rd	27.2	BR	623
9.0	R	50 ☹	28.8	L	50
9.7	L	611, St Louis Rd	29.1	R	623, Rokeby Rd
16.9	L	734, Snickersville Turnpike	32.7	L	710, Rectortown Rd
			39.4	L	to parking

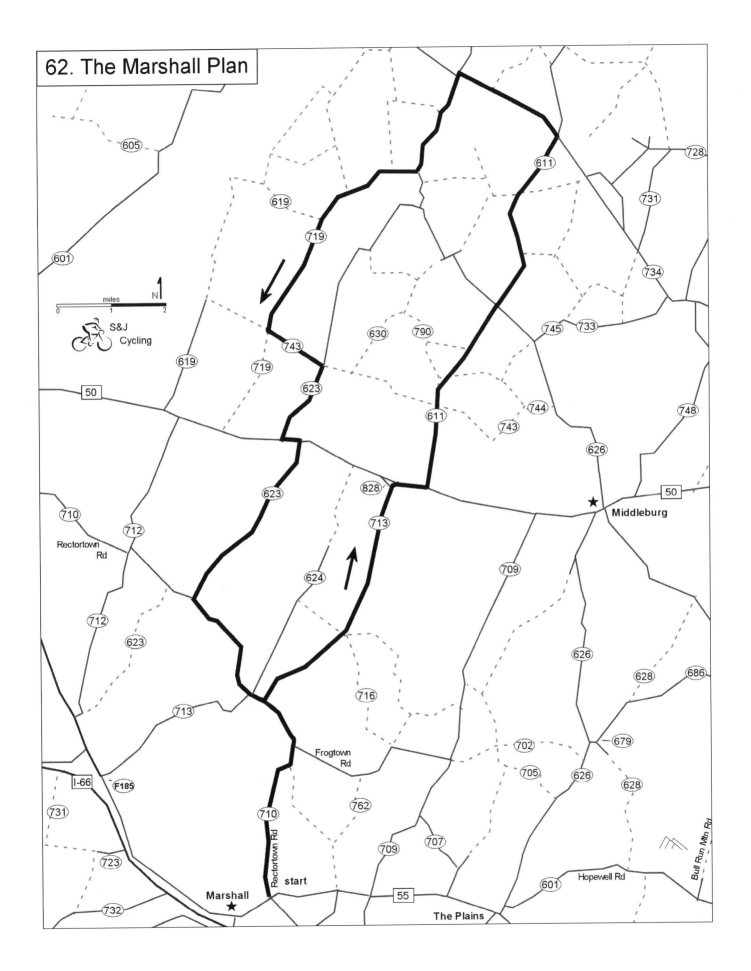

62. The Marshall Plan

S&J Cycling

63. Stormin' the Gap

Distance:	47 or 55 miles
Rating:	IV
Start:	Marshall Community Library in Marshall, Va.

55 Mile Ride

0.0		North on 710 from parking
4.2	L	713 in **Rectortown**
4.6	S	713 at fork
7.8	L	F-185
10.4 ☞*	R	732
14.9	R	635
18.2	S	635 in **Hume**, crossing 688
25.5	R	522, Zachary Taylor Rd at T ☹
31.3		Becomes Commerce Ave in **Front Royal**
32.9	R	Happy Creek Rd at light. Becomes 624
36.5	R	647, Dismal Hollow Rd
39.5	L	55
49.3	R	731 at T
49.4	L	F-184 after crossing under I-66
51.3	L	723
51.4	R	F-185. Becomes Main St in **Marshall**
54.6	L	710 to parking

*47 Mile Ride

0.0		South on 710 from parking
0.1	R	Main St at SL
2.2	L	732

Join 55-mile ride after cue at 10.4

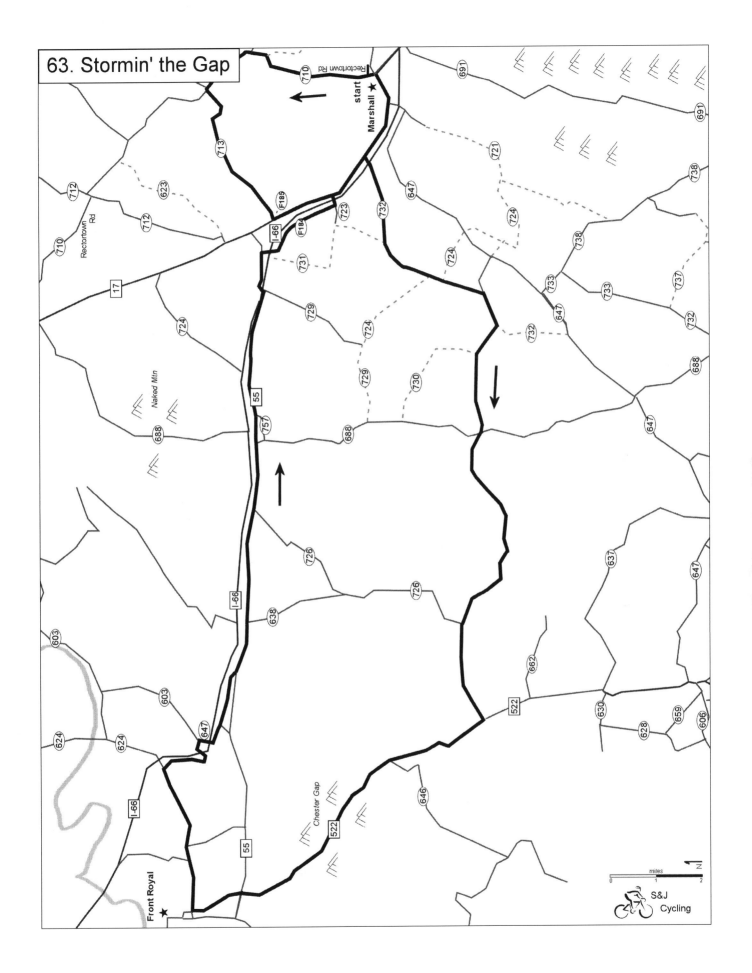

63. Stormin' the Gap

64. The Piedmont Pig Ride

Distance:	54 miles
Rating:	V
Start:	Marshall Community Library in Marshall, Va.

0.0		South on 710 from parking
0.1	S	710, crossing Main St at SL
1.2	R	691, Carter's Run after crossing I-66
9.6	L	691
12.0	R	691, Old Waterloo Rd
14.1	R	688, Leeds Manor Rd (unmarked) in **Waterloo**
19.8		**Orlean** (store)
26.1		**Hume**
31.5	L	688
31.6		Cross 55 and go under I-66
38.3	L	17, Winchester Rd ☹
40.2	R	50, John Mosby Hwy
43.6	R	712, Delaplane Grade Rd
46.3	L	710, Rectortown Rd
54.4	L	parking

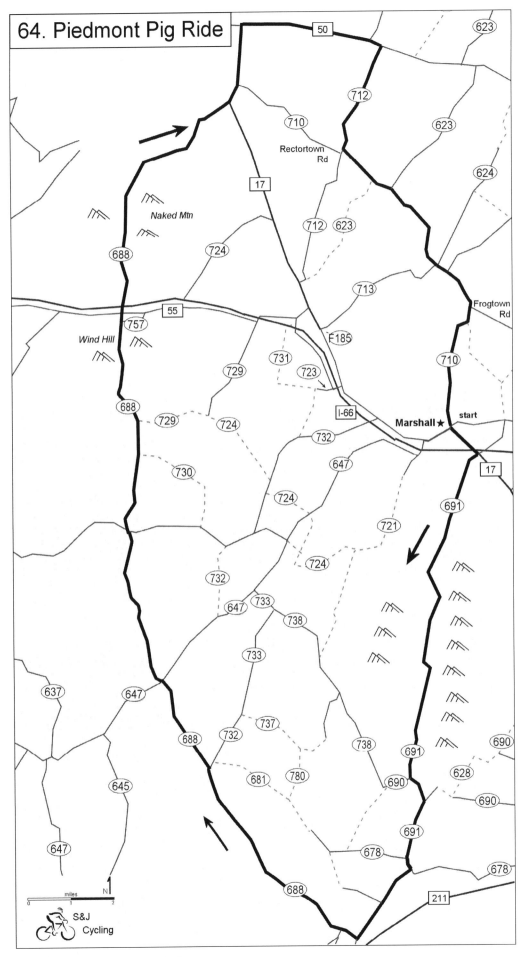

64. Piedmont Pig Ride

65. The Blue Ridger

Distance:	51 or **56** miles
Rating:	V
Start:	Marshall Community Library in Marshall, Va.

56 Mile Ride

0.0		North on 710 from parking
6.6	R	623, Rokeby Rd
10.3	L	50, John Mosby Hwy ☹
10.7	R	623, Willisville Rd
12.3	BL	743, Millville Rd
13.6	R	719, Green Garden Rd. Becomes Airmont Rd
20.3	L	734, Snickersville Tpke in **Airmont** (store)
24.2	L	7 at T ☹
24.8	L	601, Blue Ridge Mountain Rd at top of gap
36.1	L	50, John Mosby Hwy at SS ☹ ☞*
37.1	R	671

37.3	R	701 (to head south)
38.0	R	17 at T ☹
39.4	R	688 (2nd climb)
46.2	L	55, after crossing under I-66
50.4	R	731 at T; 55 goes left
50.5	L	F184, after crossing under I-66
52.5	L	723 to cross over I-66
52.6	R	F185 at T; becomes Main St in **Marshall**
55.9	L	710, Rectortown Rd at SL (store)
56.0	R	to parking

*51 Mile Ride

37.4	S	TRO 50 at 17
40.8	R	712, Delaplane Grade Rd
43.5	L	710, Rectortown Rd
51.6	L	parking

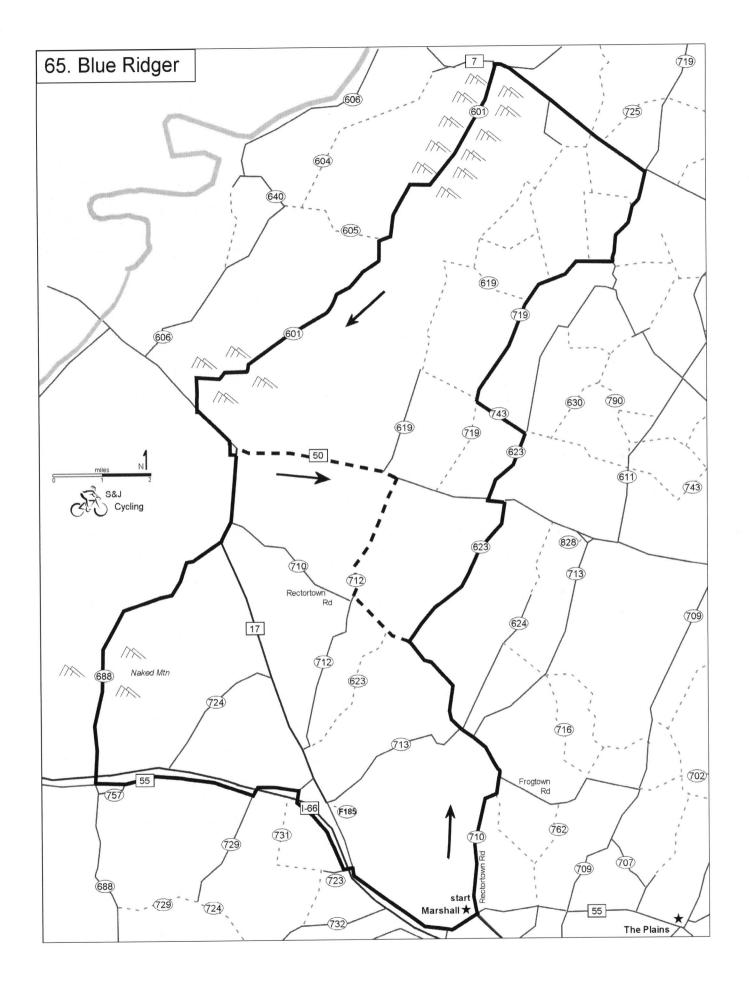

65. Blue Ridger

7

719

606

725

601

604

640

605

619

719

606

601

743

619

719

623

630

790

50

611

743

S&J
Cycling

710

712

828

Rectortown
Rd

623

713

709

17

624

688 *Naked Mtn*

712

623

724

716

713

55

Frogtown
Rd

702

757

I-66 F185

731

762

710

729

709 707

688

723

start
Marshall ★

Rectortown Rd

729 724

732

55

★

The Plains

About the Authors

Scott and his wife Sarah live in Arlington, VA. Scott has been roaming the area on a variety of Cannondales (and a Bike Friday) for 10 years, most of the time with Jim.

Jim and his wife Mary live in Oakton, VA, along with their three children, Matthew, Sally, and Emily. Jim continually hopes that one of his children will become a dedicated road cyclist and that he beats Scott up a hill now and then.

Team Cholesterol 2005 (Scott, Michael, Sarang, Jay and Jim).